THE LITTLE BOOK OF
SATANISM

T0001628

THE LITTLE BOOK OF
$ATANISM

A GUIDE TO SATANIC HISTORY, CULTURE & WISDOM

LA CARMINA

FOREWORD BY
LUCIEN GREAVES
OF THE SATANIC TEMPLE

Published by:
Ulysses Press
PO Box 3440
Berkeley, CA 94703
www.ulyssespress.com

ISBN: 978-1-64604-422-1
Library of Congress Control Number: 2022936186

Printed in the United States by Kingery Printing Company
2 4 6 8 10 9 7 5 3

Acquisitions editor: Casie Vogel
Managing editor: Claire Chun
Editor: Cathy Cambron
Proofreader: Michele Anderson
Front cover design: Raquel Castro
Interior design: what!design @ whatweb.com
Production: Winnie Liu
Cover artwork: pattern from Vecteezy.com
Interior artwork: shutterstock.com images on page 34 © joshimerbin, page 38 © Martial Red, page 41 © Digishare, page 42 © Ahmed Abuelnaga, page 43 © robin.ph; pages 39 and 40 downloaded from Wikimedia Commons

"Those who consider the Devil to be
a partisan of Evil and angels to be warriors
for Good accept the demagogy of the angels.
Things are clearly more complicated."

—MILAN KUNDERA,
THE BOOK OF LAUGHTER AND FORGETTING

CONTENTS

FOREWORD 9

INTRODUCTION: SYMPATHY FOR THE DEVIL 17

PART ONE
Please Allow Me to Introduce Myself 21

PART TWO
Historical Satanism—the Middle Ages to the
Early Twentieth Century 45

PART THREE
Modern Satanism—the Mid to Late Twentieth Century.....75

PART FOUR
Satanism Today—the Twenty-First Century.......................107

CONCLUSION
Your Own Personal Satan...131

SELECTED BIBLIOGRAPHY 135

TIMELINE OF SATANISM 137

ABOUT THE AUTHOR 142

FOREWORD

BY LUCIEN GREAVES

When I seek to confront misconceptions about Satanism, the immediate assumption is that I will scrutinize the improbable, and already long debunked, conspiracy theories about a secretive, cannibalistic worldwide cabal—once the paranoid fantasy of 1980s daytime talk shows and again finding a credulous audience in today's deluded QAnon movement. These confrontations with conspiracy theories necessarily focus on what Satanism is *not*, delving into the evolution of the folklore of "Satanic Ritual Abuse," historic witch hunts, and the discrediting of Satanic Panic fictions sold as "true stories"—such as the influential 1980 mass-market best seller *Michelle Remembers*, which purported to be a true account of "recovered memories" of Satanic cult crimes.

As horrific as Satanic Panic narratives are, with their insistence that "real" Satanism is necessarily cruel, bloodthirsty, and antihuman, there are more insidious misconceptions of Satanism that are pervasive among more reasonable minds and that are less vulnerable to an appeal to critical thinking.

After Malcolm Jarry and I cofounded The Satanic Temple in 2013, our demands that Satanism be represented in public forums where religious expression has been put on display led many of those who have been concerned by the erosion of separation of church and state to assume that we had found a "loophole" in religious liberty laws. It is a loophole, they believe, that we exploit to underscore the hypocrisy of religious zealots who vehemently fight back against Satanists having equal access to a forum that the theocrats themselves secured access to in an appeal to freedom of speech.

The fact that modern Satanism is largely nontheistic, with the majority of self-identified Satanists openly disavowing belief in a literal Satan, has contributed to the notion that those who self-identify as Satanists do so, first and foremost, to best elicit hypocritical responses from the free speech theocrats. After all, the First Amendment is meant to guarantee that the government cannot engage in viewpoint discrimination by allowing one religious voice in a public forum while excluding another. How better to confront the theocrats' efforts to expand religious privileges than to show them that their efforts are aiding the proliferation of the religious identity that they like the least?

To many, unfortunately, this kind of Satanic public activism appears to be an elaborate, clever prank. To this audience, the paranoid fictions of the Satanic Panic are clearly bogus, and the homicidal cults once said to be concealing backward messages in heavy metal music, while indoctrinating children through Dungeons & Dragons role-playing sessions, obviously never existed. However, nontheistic Satanism appears to these observers less as the truth about Satanism as a religious identity and more as another narrative about a religion that does not really exist—a convenient label for a certain type of atheist activist who knows how to fight Christian nationalists on their own terms.

Media outlets that have covered the activities of The Satanic Temple have often shamelessly given substantial airtime to our opposition without trying to gain any understanding of who we are, or what we are doing, by seeking any comment from us at all. Legal experts, asked by journalists to measure the credibility of some

11

of the lawsuits we have filed in defense of our religious rights, almost universally exhibit a total failure to learn the first thing about Satanism before weighing in.

Thus, with no understanding of the fact that The Satanic Temple has more than half a million followers worldwide, with an ever-growing number of active congregations that engage in regular activities and services, these "experts" will often state that our status as a bona fide religion is still in dispute. Apparently ignorant of the Internal Revenue Service's recognition of The Satanic Temple's tax-exempt status in 2019 and unaware that a federal judge affirmed our undeniable religious authenticity in an equal access dispute ruling in 2020, legal scholars still treat the sincerity of our claims as an open question.

All of this, of course, ignores the large and growing subculture of individuals for whom Satanism is a meaningful religious identity, regardless of the reaction this identity provokes in other people. The "blasphemous" iconography of Satanism is, for most Satanists, a declaration of personal liberation from traditional theistic institutions and the sometimes arbitrary restrictions they impose on their followers, rather than a calculated

12

insult directed at faithful believers with the intention to offend. And, far from being a mere "loophole" or "prank," meant only to "raise awareness" of Christian nationalist hypocrisy, our demands for equal access in public forums are a legitimate battle to preserve true religious liberty.

The stakes in the Satanist battle for religious liberty are high, and the ramifications for the outcomes extend far beyond those who identify as Satanists and those who actively oppose us. Will we allow the civic capacities of certain religious identities to be expanded while excluding others? Are claims of conscience to be respected only when presented by certain approved faiths? Indeed, are claims of conscience to be invalidated if not attached to archaic supernaturalist traditions? If public officials are able to deny basic civil liberties to Satanists, even if they do wrongly assume that Satanism is a provocation rather than an authentic religious identity, whom might they target next?

There is a critical need for handy resources that can disabuse the public of misconceptions about Satanism. The best way to do so is to educate people about what Satanism is, rather than continually explaining what it is not. Although The Satanic Temple was founded only in 2013, a long history charts the evolution of modern Satanism from Milton's poetic elaboration of the ultimate rebel against tyranny, to the literary Satanists of the nineteenth century, to the theatrical Satanism of Anton LaVey's Church of Satan in the 1960s.

In making clearer and more accessible histories of modern Satanism, the hope is that broader audiences can begin to understand what Satanism really means to those who practice it. Perhaps it will become clearer to readers why Satanism is a nonnegotiable identity to some; indeed, it is their religion. And, perhaps, for a still more aspirational hope, there are some readers, with religious views that they believe to be diametrically opposed to Satanic values, who will nonetheless understand that equality for Satanists is worth defending so that we do not submit ourselves to the far greater evil of an arbitrarily regulated religious consciousness. There is even the hope that some, of traditional religious faiths, can learn about Satanism and conceive of a world in which they—under a different set of circumstances—could find Satanism to be a source of comfort and community as well.

It is my hope that general audiences can learn about modern Satanism and, even if they would never identify as Satanists themselves, can nonetheless see the individualistic, humanistic, and plain human motives of real-world Satanists. Perhaps even a few faithful believers will learn about the Satanist struggle and come to conclude that "there but for the grace of God go I."

—Lucien Greaves
Cofounder and spokesperson of The Satanic Temple

Salem, Massachusetts
May 2022

INTRODUCTION: SYMPATHY FOR THE DEVIL

In the popular imagination, Satanism plays out like a scene from a B horror movie. Picture ghoulish figures in black cloaks, chanting "Hail Satan!" as they conduct a blood sacrifice on a pentagram for the Prince of Darkness. Some church leaders and conspiracy theorists insist that a cabal of literal Devil worshippers is lurking in the shadows, wishing nothing more than to rain torment upon innocents in pursuit of an insidious world-dominating agenda.

In reality, the practice of Satanism is far removed from these lurid fantasies. Modern Satanists are nonviolent and for the most part nontheistic, meaning they don't believe in the actual existence of the Devil. Rather, Satan—the fallen angel who defied God—is a metaphor for the revolt against superstition and arbitrary author-ity. Like the antihero of *Paradise Lost*, Satanists proudly identify as outsiders who dare to stand up for knowl-edge, reason, and justice.

The Little Book of Satanism aims to dispel the widespread misconceptions and conspiracy theories about Satanists. Starting from the Devil's earliest origins, I detail the "mark of the beast" on cultural and historic movements over the centuries, which have informed the sincerely held beliefs and practices of Satanists today. Time and time again, the goat-headed one has been made the scapegoat for social issues, from medieval witch trials to the 1980s Satanic Panic. Modern Satanists, however, have flipped the script by associating the Devil with a positive and meaningful religious identity.

Satanists take very different journeys on what is consid-ered the "Left-Hand Path." Some are members of the two most prominent organizations, the Church of Satan and The Satanic Temple. Others belong to small groups or have an individualized practice based on a variety of source material. Practitioners also express their sincere religious identification in diverse ways, with some engaging in rituals or community activism.

Rather than try to narrowly define a "true Satanism," this book invites you to understand the motivations and affirmative values that are consistent among many self-declared modern Satanists. These include:

⚸ Rejecting irrational dogma, tyrannical authority, and conventional moral judgments

⚸ Championing nonconformity, empathy, and personal expression—including elements considered transgressive by the status quo

⚸ Pursuing knowledge through a rational, science-based approach that rejects superstition

⚸ Relating to the figure of Satan as a meaningful symbol of individuality and rebellion

⚸ Engaging in some form of Satanic doctrine, practice, community, or organization

This being a "little book," it will be impossible to cover all the variations of the movement, including theistic Satanists and outliers with more esoteric beliefs. Instead, I focus on the themes and individuals most relevant to Satanism as it is generally expressed today. As the saying goes, "the Devil is in the details"—so if a subject piques your interest, I encourage you to examine it further through the sources in the Selected Bibliography.

Now is the time to discard malevolent stereotypes about Satanists, and take a truthful look at the history and ideas of the movement through the ages. In the spirit of Lucifer the adversary, I hope you'll be inspired by Satanism's affirmative values that courageously oppose injustice and speak up for nonconformity, free inquiry, and personal liberty.

Ave Satanas!

—La Carmina

LaCarmina.com / @LaCarmina

PART ONE

LEASE ALLOW ME TO INTRODUCE MYSELF

THE DEVIL'S PREDECESSORS

For as long as humans have been able to tell one another stories, there have been tales of malevolent and chaotic spirits. The world was full of distressing events that people could not understand—whether it was famine by blights or deaths from mysterious internal causes. To explain life's most fearful elements, cultures world-wide developed the idea of superhuman beings that sometimes preyed on humanity and engineered misfor-tunes. As a means of countering these malicious forces, many invoked protection from benevolent gods through prayers and rituals. Such early spiritual traditions also helped uphold the social order: whenever there was conflict, those in power could put the blame on demons.

Cultures and religions around the globe have long imagined Devil-like figures—from the Mayan death gods that lorded over a frightful underworld, to China's Yanluo Wang, who judged the deceased before the gates of Hell. The roots of Satanism, however, are embedded in the character of Satan in Judeo-Christian theology. But the Prince of Darkness wasn't created in a vacuum: his conceptualization drew from numerous faiths and folklores, and these influences were crossbred and elaborated over the centuries to form the Devil we know today.

In particular, the religions of the ancient Near East directly shaped the development of the biblical Satan. Babylonian and Canaanite myths spoke of a creator god who battled a sea monster, and a variation of this narrative later appeared in the biblical tale of Leviathan. The Egyptians had a rich pantheon of morally ambiguous deities, meaning that each god had qualities of both good and evil. Set—the god of violence and disorder—skewed closer to the latter and likely inspired the personification of Satan. Ancient Egyptians also conceived of a Hell-like underworld called *duat* where souls were judged after death. Jackal-headed Anubis weighed human hearts against a feather, and those that were heavier were tortured and consumed by fire or hungry demons.

Likewise, the ancient Greeks had morally ambiguous gods and believed that the dead were ferried across the River Styx to the subterranean abode of Hades. Many of Satan's visual qualities can be traced to Pan, the goatlike god of fertility and shepherds, who indulged in carnal pleasures in the wild.

Perhaps the Devil's closest forebear comes from Zoroastrianism, which is the oldest recorded religion to conceive of the world in dualist terms (the eternal opposition of good versus evil and Heaven versus Hell). The Persian prophet Zoroaster, or Zarathustra, taught of a supreme creator god, Ahura Mazda, which stood for goodness and light and was supported by heavenly deities. His antithesis was the destructive Angra Mainyu, or Ahriman, who dwelled in darkness with his demonic army and sometimes appeared in the form of a snake. Zoroastrianism taught that humans had free will and could choose which of the two to follow. Those who hailed Ahriman were doomed to fall into an eternal darkness of "bad food and lamentation."

SATAN'S GENESIS IN THE BIBLE

Over time, this pantheon of dark spiritual progenitors directly and indirectly contributed to the emergence of the Judeo-Christian Satan. Although the concept of the Devil came to be integral to Christian interpretations of the Bible, it is difficult to find a coherent description of his biography, personality, and role in its books. Rather, Satan's story was assembled over the millennia as theologians and writers scoured the scattered references in biblical passages and reinterpreted them through the lenses of other doctrines and legends.

Satan makes his debut in the texts that ended up forming the Hebrew Bible, or Tanakh, which was written approximately between 1200 and 165 BCE. (The Christian Old Testament contains nearly the same materials but arranged in a different order.) In these early works, he is not the powerful ruler of Hell but merely an angelic servant of Yahweh, the God of Israel and Judah. Satan's name is derived from the Hebrew root *śtn*, which refers to one who acts as an adversary or accuser. Rather than describing an individual named Satan, the Hebrew Bible used the noun *hassatan* ("the satan") to mean an adversary, as well as to describe any angel in an oppositional role.

In the book of Numbers, Yahweh sends "the satan" to block the path of Balaam, a non-Israelite prophet who embarks on a journey in opposition to divine will. The angelic emissary blocks the path of Balaam's donkey, which bolts off the path and lies down to avoid the invisible nemesis. Since Balaam cannot see *hassatan,* the prophet grows angry and whips his animal for being a "smart ass." That's when "the satan" reveals himself and explains his divine role as an adversary. Awed, Balaam repents and agrees to do as the Lord commands.

In the book of Job, *hassatan* is an officer in Yahweh's heavenly council and demonstrates his role as an objector for the first time. "The satan" questions whether the devout and prosperous Job is serving the Lord only because the man is blessed with divine favor. With the Lord's permission, "the satan" tests Job's faith by taking his wealth, killing his children in a mighty wind, and inflicting sores all over his body. Despite his immense suffering, Job stays loyal to God and his good fortune is restored, proving *hassatan* wrong.

Satan becomes a proper name in the New Testament, which was written approximately between 50 and 100 ACE. The Scriptures describe a single adversary who still operates under divine control but now has a greater and more powerful role as the enemy of Jesus Christ and humankind. The Devil appears to the son of God during his fast in the wilderness and tempts him to turn stones into loaves of bread. Later, the Devil takes Jesus to a mountaintop and promises Jesus worldly power if he bows down to Satan. Each time, Jesus calls out, "Away with you, Satan!" and banishes his tempter.

The book of Revelation gives the fullest account of Satan as the harbinger of evil, portraying him through the terrifying visions of the apocalyptic war that he wages against God and his angels. The Devil appears in the hideous form of a great red dragon and gives authority to a beast that comes from the sea and one that comes from the earth. The latter has two horns and is described as the false prophet associated with the number 666. (While most people think it is the Devil's number, 666 was the number of the beast and works out in Hebrew numerology to signify Nero, the cruel Roman emperor who persecuted early Christians.) At the end of Revelation, the archangel Michael conquers Satan and casts him down from Heaven. The Devil is bound for one thousand years, then is briefly set free and wages a final battle against God. Ultimately, Satan and his demons are defeated and hurled into the lake of fire and brimstone to spend eternity there.

Satan's character is barely sketched out in the Bible. Many now-widespread ideas about his origins and evil-doings were developed later through extrabiblical texts, theological treatises, and folk and morality tales. For instance, in the Jewish tradition, the cunning serpent that tempts Eve is simply a talking snake. However, starting in the first century CE, some Christians reinterpreted book of Genesis to suggest that the serpent was the Devil in disguise, enticing Adam and Eve to taste the fruit from the tree of knowledge.

This retroactive reading of the Scriptures helps explain a paradox: if God is omnipotent and wholly good, then why is there suffering in the world that he made and has the power to change? Christians can come to terms with this contradiction by blaming Satan for leading innocents astray. Since humans have free will, they may decide to follow the Devil into wickedness. However, Christians believe Satan is not God's equal and can operate only within the limits set forth by his divine will. In other words, God allows the villain to amuse himself on Earth for some time, but the Devil will inevitably be conquered and confined to Hell.

In contrast to this dominant narrative, a modern Satanist can consider the same Genesis passages and metaphorically interpret them from an empowering, feminist point of view. This alternative reading suggests that Eve considered herself equal to her husband and sought knowledge unfairly denied to her by God. By courageously eating the fruit, she refused to be subjugated by arbitrary authority. From this perspective, Eve should be commended for listening to the Devil's wise words and standing up for herself, rather than be disparaged for her "original sin."

Besides the Devil himself, there are a few other figures from the Judeo-Christian tradition who are linked to Satanism:

⚹ The Antichrist (Jesus's archenemy) is mentioned in the New Testament's First and Second Epistles of John, and his life story is elaborated in early medieval treatises. Generally, the Antichrist is considered to be an incarnation of Satan, or his son, or the chief of his army. The false prophet presents himself as the Messiah, deceives humanity, and reigns over the world for a short time until he is defeated in the Second Coming of Christ.

⚹ Lilith, a female demon in Judaic folklore, is known as Adam's first wife, who refused to lie beneath him. Other legends say she defied her husband and coupled with the archangel Samael or became the consort of Satan. In the late nineteenth century, some writers and philosophers hailed Lilith for her independence and unabashed sexuality. Today, many Satanists consider her a positive female symbol.

✡ Islam originated in the seventh century, and some of its theology can be traced to Judaism and Christianity. The Koran portrays Iblis, or Shaitan—leader of grotesque demons and tempter of humans—as a minor irritant to Allah and was condemned to Hell for disobedience. Later, Iblis received permission from Allah to try to mislead Adam and his descendants but never had power over them. Islam also has an Antichrist figure called the Dajjal, a deceitful Messiah who is blind in his right eye.

It is important to note that most Satanists do not believe in the existence of any of these supernatural figures, let alone worship them. Regardless, Satanists may find insight in a diabolical analysis of biblical materials that refutes the Christian narrative that many grew up with. Rereading the Scriptures can help them contextualize a universe that felt imposed upon them and find resolve in the Devil and his infernal comrades.

WHAT IS SATAN'S NAME?

The Hebrew root of Satan, śtn, was usually translated in Greek to *diabolos*, "accuser" or "slanderer." When *diabolos* was eventually translated into English, "the Devil" was spawned. Today, in common usage, "Satan" and "the Devil" are used interchangeably.

Around the first century, "Lucifer" became known as Satan's primordial name before he was cast out of Heaven. A passage from the book of Isaiah refers to the fall of a king of Babylon: "How are you fallen from Heaven / O Day Star, son of Dawn!... to the depths of the pit." When translated into Latin from the Greek version of the Old Testament, "Day Star" or "Morning Star" becomes Lucifer, or "bringer of light" (a name also associated with the celestial body that the Romans called Venus). Theologians linked these two lines to a comment from Jesus in Luke—"I saw Satan fall like lightning from Heaven"—forming a backstory about how Lucifer and his rebel angels staged a failed coup against God. Much later, the nineteenth-century Romantic writers found inspiration in the tale and reframed it to depict Satan as a glorious antihero who rose up against the tyranny of Heaven.

In the Middle Ages, however, Lucifer was sometimes treated as an entity separate and distinct from the Devil. Later, some nineteenth- and twentieth-century esoteric groups saw Lucifer as a positive entity and Satan as a negative one, or thought the two represented different human tendencies. Some modern Satanists make similar distinctions and prefer to self-identify as Luciferians. But for the most part, Lucifer is identified as the prideful Satan in the Bible and in literature about his fall from Heaven.

Here is where the story gets complicated. The Devil is associated with other infernal names, some of which are conflated with dark mythological figures from the ancient Near East. Perhaps you may have heard of Beelzebub ("Lord of the Flies"), Leviathan, Mephistopheles, and Belial.

Different texts—the Bible, medieval plays, demonic grimoires—have differing or fluid conceptions of these diabolical names and their relations to one another. There aren't enough pages in this book to go through the etymology of each, so suffice it to say that the appellations are sometimes used to specify Satan's alter egos but usually refer to his demonic agents or lieutenants. The main idea communicated by these names is that malevolent spirits were organized behind an evil leader and went into the world under his command to wreak havoc.

SPEAK OF THE DEVIL: SATAN'S MANY NAMES

Beyond the ones outlined in this section, there are many other colorful and endearing nicknames for our fallen angel. These monikers include:

- ⚝ The Devil
- ⚝ Lucifer
- ⚝ Beelzebub ("Lord of the Flies")
- ⚝ Leviathan
- ⚝ Mephistopheles
- ⚝ Mammon
- ⚝ Mastema
- ⚝ Belial
- ⚝ Baal
- ⚝ Azazel
- ⚝ Abaddon
- ⚝ Apollyon
- ⚝ Asmodeus
- ⚝ Astaroth
- ⚝ Prince of Darkness
- ⚝ Father of Lies
- ⚝ The Deceiver
- ⚝ Old Horny
- ⚝ Old Scratch
- ⚝ Old Nick
- ⚝ Old Hairy

WHAT DOES SATAN LOOK LIKE?

To dress as Satan for Halloween, a person would likely put on red face paint and horns, tie on a cape, attach a long barbed tail, and hold a pitchfork. But the Devil has as many faces as he has names, and his visual identity reflects the ways humans have contemplated him over time.

The Bible does not detail Satan's appearance, so artists from the early Middle Ages drew from a variety of sources in envisioning his physical features. The book of Revelation does describe Satan's incarnation as a scarlet dragon with horns—qualities that have become signatures of Old Horny. Set, the Devil's Egyptian antecedent, was similarly associated with serpents and depicted in

Figure 1. The red dragon of Revelation, seen as an incarnation of Satan.

red to convey the scorching heat of the desert. With his lolling tongue and snakes issuing from his body, a minor Egyptian fertility god named Bes may have also provided inspiration.

The first known depiction of Satan is a mosaic from the year 520 CE at Sant'Apollinare Nuovo in Ravenna, Italy. Portrayed as a haloed angel, he sits to the left of Jesus with a group of goats before him. An angel sits on Christ's right, behind a flock of sheep. The work references the Gospel of Matthew's avowal that Jesus will separate the sheep from the goats on Judgment Day. The horned beasts represent sin and disobedience, so they are sent to Satan's side.

For this reason, Satan is often shown with goats or as a horned and hoofed deity. The connection is strengthened by the book of Leviticus, which describes how a goat took on the sins of the Israelites and was thrown over a cliff, becoming the first scapegoat. Medieval artists thought the Devil was cut from the same cloth as the Greek pastoral god Pan, so they drew him as a similarly lecherous and hairy beast. Cernunnos, the lustful Celtic god of the forest, may have also influenced representations of the horned one. Finally, Satan is associated with the goatlike Baphomet, whom we'll meet in the following section.

As for the Devil's pitchfork, it is reminiscent of the trident used by Poseidon, the Greek god of the sea. The tenth-century Muiredach's High Cross, located in a ruined monastery in Ireland, is possibly the first carving to show Satan using a pitchfork to herd the damned into Hell and torture them. Peasants would have been able to identify with this pastoral imagery, as they used similar tools to prod their farm animals.

Most people were illiterate in the Middle Ages, and so they learned about Christian doctrine from carvings, stained glass, and mosaics. By giving a face to the Deceiver, church leaders were able to personify and communicate the abstract notion of evil—and reinforce a belief in the Devil. They encouraged artists to depict Satan as the frightening opposite of the beatific God: a screaming and sensual beast sheathed in darkness, typically with bat wings, fur, fangs, claws, horns, and hooves. For example, in their fifteenth-century Last Judgment triptychs, Giotto, Fra Angelico, and Hans Memling painted the Devil as a black-skinned monster devouring lost souls who tumbled into hellfire.

With the dawn of the Enlightenment, a seventeenth- and eighteenth-century movement that valued science and rationality, most people no longer thought of Satan as an immediate manifestation of supernatural power to be feared in daily life. Instead, many artists drew him as a rebel that stood valiantly against ecclesiastical authority. Nineteenth-century artists Eugène Delacroix and William Blake showed their sympathy for the Devil by illustrating him as a classic muscled hero. Other art from this time depicted Satan in the form of a kind old man or a dandy trickster. The Devil was also imagined as a sexually attractive figure, notably in Guillaume Geefs's 1848 sculpture *Lucifer of Liège:* the toned and bat-winged angel is nearly naked and runs a hand seductively through his long hair. Today, Satan's iconography runs the gamut of influences from past centuries—and he may even take on cute or kitschy forms.

WHAT ARE THE SYMBOLS OF SATANISM?

Modern Satanism is associated with symbols such as the pentagram and the number 666 (discussed on page

27), which can be found on jewelry, tattoos, album covers, Goth clothing, home decor, and more. As Satanism is a syncretistic religion, its symbolism emerged over time from a variety of sources, including demonology, alchemy, and other systems of belief. For many Satanists, these "marks of the beast" embody shock or blasphemy, as well as a declaration of their personal independence from superstition. Such symbols are often proudly worn or displayed to express a religious identification and contextualize Satanists' own life narratives.

Figure 2. The inverted pentagram.

Inverted pentagram. The five-pointed star, or pentagram, is a symbol found in numerous cultures worldwide, including the cultures of Japan and Greece, as well as faiths such as Modern Paganism and Wicca. Since ancient times, it has denoted positive qualities such as well-being. The nineteenth-century occultist Éliphas

Lévi wrote that when the pentagram is reversed (so that the two points project upward), the symbol resembles a goat's head with two horns and a triangular beard—a representation of evil. Thanks to Lévi's conjectures, the inverted pentagram became inextricably linked to Satanism and is perhaps its best-known symbol today.

Figure 3. The Sabbatic Goat.

The Sabbatic Goat, or Baphomet. In his 1856 book *Dogme et Rituel de la Haute Magie*, Lévi drew an image of the Sabbatic Goat that later became a notable symbol of Satanism. Also known as Baphomet or the Goat of Mendes, the deity is an androgynous winged humanoid goat with breasts, dark wings, a torch between its horns that represents knowledge, an upright pentagram on its forehead, and a caduceus rising from its groin. Its right arm is raised while the left points downward, in reference to the Hermetic dictum "as above, so below." To Lévi, Baphomet symbolized the equilibrium of opposites: human and animal, male and female, good and evil. The early twentieth-century occultist Aleister Crowley later adopted the symbol in his Thelemic religion to represent the union of opposing forces. Lévi's Baphomet was also used as the source image for the Devil in the 1909 Rider-Waite tarot deck. Later on, the goat-headed one became a meaningful icon for Satanists and assumed a starring role in The Satanic Temple's activism. (Later in this book, this topic, as well as the medieval origins of Baphomet, will be further discussed.)

Figure 4. Goat head in an inverted pentagram.

Goat head in an inverted pentagram. In his 1897 *Clef de la magie noire,* French occultist Stanislas de Guaïta drew an inverted pentagram in a circle that was super-imposed on a goat's head. The sigil contains the words "Samael" and "Lilith," and the outer script is Hebrew for "Leviathan." Anton LaVey saw the image without the innermost names in Maurice Bessy's *A Pictorial History of Magic and the Supernatural* (1964) and reproduced it on the cover of *The Satanic Bible* (1969). This version became known as the Sigil of Baphomet and is the official insignia of the Church of Satan. Other Satanists have used variations of de Guaïta's design to represent their affiliation. The Satanic Temple's logo, for example, is a goat's head crowned by a flaming torch within a downward-pointing pentagram, with the organization's name printed in the circle.

Figure 5. The Leviathan Cross.

The Leviathan Cross, or Brimstone Sigil. The ancient alchemical symbol for brimstone (archaic for sulfur) is the combination of an infinity sign (∞) and a double cross (†). This chemical element is linked to Satan because God cast him into a lake of fire and brimstone, according to the book of Revelation. Furthermore, influential writers such as Dante Alighieri described Hell as a sulfurous burning abode, much like a hot spring or volcano. LaVey placed this sigil, which he called the Leviathan Cross, above his Nine Satanic Statements in *The Satanic Bible*.

Figure 6. The Sigil of Lucifer.

The Sigil of Lucifer. This chalice-like design was first documented in the eighteenth-century *Grimoirium Verum* (Grimoire of Truth), which was written as a practical guide to invoking demons such as Lucifer, Beelzebub, and Astaroth. The visual design served as an instrument of invocation during a ritual. Since the sigil supposedly bestowed the presence and power of Lucifer, it became a favored symbol for Satanists.

Figure 7. The inverted cross.

Inverted cross. A symbol may have multiple meanings depending on one's cultural or philosophical underpinnings. For some Christians, this is the Cross of Saint Peter, or the Petrine Cross. To them, it represents the humility of the apostle Peter, who asked to be crucified upside down because he felt unworthy to die in the same way as Christ. However, symbols do not carry a static or intrinsic definition. In the context of Satanism, an inverted crucifix symbolizes a rejection of authoritarian Judeo-Christian doctrines and a denial of superstition and judgmentalism. Satanists might wear one to represent their affirmative values of scientific skepticism and liberation from dogma. Perhaps the first to present the symbol in this context was Eugène Vintras, an eccentric nineteenth-century cult leader who wore a robe marked with a giant upside-down cross. Vintras was rumored to take part in demonic rituals, and Lévi commented that Vintras's use of the sign hinted at his Satanic inclinations.

PART TWO

HISTORICAL SATANISM—THE MIDDLE AGES TO THE EARLY TWENTIETH CENTURY

MEDIEVAL ANTI-SATANISM AND THE KNIGHTS TEMPLAR

As Christianity spread through Europe in the Middle Ages, growing faith in an all-powerful God was accompanied by a rising fear of demonic powers aligned against the Lord and his followers. The faithful thought of the Devil not as an abstract principle, but as an active spiritual being who could cause real harm in their lives. They worried that Satan could lure innocents into sin and doom them to what Christians truly believed was eternal suffering in Hell.

The English language terms "Satanism" and "Satanist" first appear in records from the sixteenth century. However, well before this time, medieval missionaries pushed the idea of "anti-Satanism," meaning that they often accused other faiths or minorities of being in league with Old Scratch. Anyone who didn't fit the missionaries' definition of piousness—including Pagans, Jews, and Muslims—could be deemed a Devil worshipper. Furthermore, many Christians were convinced that their own denomination followed the true word of God, while dissenting groups were heretics. As a result, it was not uncommon for Catholics, Protestants, Cathars, and Anabaptists to point fingers at one another for cozying up to the Deceiver.

By the twelfth century, ecclesiastics were using aggressive means to expand and maintain their spiritual dominance, including the religious wars of the Crusades. Furthermore, Pope Innocent III established the church-wide institution of the Inquisition in 1199 to root out and punish heretics. As the personification of evil, the Devil naturally became the scapegoat for anything that those in power rejected. For instance, in the thirteenth century, rumors spread about German "Luciferians" engaging in blasphemies such as defecating on sacramental bread. Although there was never any proof of such Devil veneration, these claims had real repercussions in discrediting and ostracizing heterodox groups.

In 1128, Pope Honorius II endorsed a new military order called the Knights Templar, empowering them to protect pilgrims traveling to the Holy Land during the Crusades. As time passed, the revered Christian order accrued increasing independence and money, even though parts of the lands they were meant to protect had fallen back to the Muslims. Setting his eye on the

Knights Templar's wealth, France's King Philip IV ("Philip the Fair") ordered his inquisitors to arrest all Templars in 1307. The order was thus disbanded and their properties confiscated, and most Knights were burned at the stake.

Before executing them, the inquisitors extracted blasphemous confessions from the Knights Templar with no corroborating evidence. Under torture, the soldiers admitted to trampling and spitting on the cross, participating in sodomy, and holding meetings with Lucifer in the form of a black cat. Court records also stated that they worshipped a bearded idol with two or three faces, which they called Baphomet. Most likely, this name was a corrupted version of Mahomet, an old French word for Mohammad. Five centuries later, Éliphas Lévi drew Baphomet as the Sabbatic Goat in reference to the propaganda that cast the Templars in a diabolical light; this went on to become a significant Satanic symbol (see Part One).

DANTE'S "INFERNO" AND FAUST'S PACT

Satan's characterization continued to evolve during the European Renaissance, a period of artistic rebirth that lasted from the fourteenth century to the seventeenth. The Devil is literally at the center of *Inferno*, the first section of Dante Alighieri's 1320 epic poem, *The Divine Comedy*. The ghost of the poet Virgil guides the narrator to Hell's gate, which is inscribed, "Abandon all hope, ye who enter here!" They travel through the nine ever-narrowing circles of Hell and witness the punishments meted out to sinners on each level. (For example, gluttons are condemned to the third ring; they live in a reeking garbage heap and are mauled by Cerberus, the three-headed dog.) The ninth circle houses traitors, and God's greatest betrayer—Satan—is at the very bottom, immobilized up to his chest in a lake of ice. In a significant departure from the medieval view of Satan as a terrifyingly active evil force, Dante imagined him as a wretched and powerless creature weeping alone in the cold.

The Renaissance also birthed an influential narrative about making a pact with the Devil. Similar iterations had appeared earlier in the Middle Ages, but the story is most famously tied to the biography of Johann Georg Faust, a sixteenth-century itinerant magus who gained infamy for his magical tricks. After the death of the historical Faust, authors spun tales about how he sold his soul to Satan for worldly powers and pleasures. The best known of these dramas are Christopher Marlowe's *Doctor Faustus* (1604) and Johann Wolfgang von Goethe's *Faust* (1808–32).

In most accounts, Faust is a scholar who yearns to know the secrets of Heaven and Earth. He pledges his soul to Mephistopheles, the Devil's messenger, by signing his name in blood. Mephistopheles then takes Faust on thrilling and sensual adventures through the realms. The Renaissance stories have a moral tone: at the end of Marlowe's *Faustus*, the protagonist is dragged offstage to Hell. However, Enlightenment writers envisioned Faust as a curious, intelligent, and heroic fellow. In Goethe's retelling, the man signed away his soul, went on adventures in far-off places—and still wound up in Heaven. The trope about making a pact with the Devil remains popular today and can be seen in contemporary movies, TV shows, and novels.

DEMONIC POSSESSION AND EXORCISMS

While Faust willingly gave away his soul, another narrative exists about innocents who are unwillingly overcome by the Devil or one of his demons. Signs of demonic possession include growling or shrieking blasphemies, distorting one's face, bulging out one's eyes, contorting the limbs, or vomiting profusely. As even the pious could have their bodies demonically occupied, the possessed would not be considered morally culpable or responsible for their actions while in this distressing state.

Many cultures worldwide have a spiritual tradition of evicting demons or evil spirits from a body in a ritual known as an exorcism. The Christian version dates back to the time of Jesus, as the Bible speaks of him casting out wicked spirits from the possessed. The term "exorcist" emerged in the early second century to describe a church member who could invoke the power of God to banish the Devil or demons. The exorcist might wield prayers, a crucifix, holy water, or other consecrated materials to evict the unholy squatter.

Although exorcisms peaked during the era of the witch trials (described next), they are still performed in earnest today. Non-Christians might write off the custom as harmless playacting for the sake of psychological release. However, the practice can turn deadly when misguided people take it into their own hands. For example, in 2019, a six-year-old Arizona boy was drowned by his father, who attempted to deliver him from evil by forcing water into his mouth. The following year, a four-year-old Missouri girl died after being beaten and dunked in an icy pond to drive out a demon. Unfortunately, many other innocents have become entangled in Satanic accusations over the years and lost their lives because of them—perhaps most appallingly during the European witch purges.

WITCH HUNTS

In the fourteenth century, Europe entered a period of crisis brought on by the Black Death, the Great Famine, and a series of violent revolts and dynastic wars. The Catholic Church was also divided by the Western Schism, in which three rival popes with loyal followings laid claim to the title of supreme pontiff. During these turbulent times, worries about the Devil's influence grew among the embattled populace—and many church leaders seized the opportunity to consolidate their influence and eradicate unorthodox beliefs. These brewing social anxieties bubbled over into accusations of witchcraft, resulting in large-scale persecutions throughout north central Europe and colonial America that waxed and waned until around 1700.

Malleus Maleficarum (Hammer of the Witches), a witch-hunting manual published in 1486 by two German inquisitors, was a major impetus for the craze. The book codified the notion that witches and warlocks were followers of Satan and actively colluded with him to rain death and destruction upon humans. *Malleus Maleficarum* voyeuristically described witches lying half-naked in the fields, copulating with invisible demons with their legs in the air. At night, they flew on brooms to join the witches' Sabbath, an obscene ritual during which participants engaged in orgies, ate babies, trampled on crosses, and lined up to kiss the Devil's backside. Some witch hunter texts from this time imaginatively described Satan's member (enormous and red, or twisted and scaly with a pointy tip) and his ejaculate (it was ice cold).

As these fearful ideas took hold, more and more innocents found themselves accused of practicing black magic in the name of Satan. If a farmer's livestock fell ill, he might put the blame on spells cast by an eccentric female neighbor. Catholic leaders, Protestant clergy, and secular authorities alike investigated these charges by looking for physical signs, such as birthmarks or third nipples, which supposedly proved the accused was a witch. Since witchcraft was considered an extraordinary crime, interrogators were permitted to torture victims by, for example, stretching them on the rack or forcing them to sit on spiked or red-hot metal chairs. If they succumbed to the pain and confessed, then they were found guilty and burned at the stake, hanged, or beheaded.

About 80 percent of the accused were women. As supposed descendants of Eve, women were considered more susceptible to Satan's influence, as well as to lust and vanity. Most of those targeted were older spinsters or pariahs, especially those who had disabilities or defied social norms and were deemed "difficult." Previously respected healers and herbalists could easily be denounced as sorceresses. While it is challenging for researchers to determine exact numbers, many estimate that fifty thousand to one hundred thousand witches were tried and executed in Europe. Some regions also conducted werewolf trials, which persecuted mostly men for allegedly shape-shifting into wolves and eating children under the Devil's command.

In the mid to late 1600s, a mania of witchcraft delusions swept through Puritan colonies on the East Coast of North America. These anxieties came to a head in 1692 in Salem, Massachusetts. Tituba, an indigenous Caribbean slave, entertained the girls she served with harmless voodoo tales and fortune-telling games from her homeland. Suddenly, the girls began exhibiting strange behaviors such as convulsing, speaking in tongues, and barking. A doctor suggested that Satan's influence was to blame, and word spread that Tituba was a witch.

The slave confessed under duress to entering into a pact with a hairy, long-nosed Devil. She said she saw nine other signatures scrawled in blood in Satan's book. Soon, other marginalized women (and some men) were tried for witchcraft, including elderly and homeless individuals—and many were sentenced to death. The colony's governor put an end to the witch hysteria in 1693 after his own wife was accused. By then, nineteen had been hanged, one man had been pressed to death with heavy stones, and several others had died in prison.

Historians have suggested a mix of explanations for the Salem witch trials. Certainly, rising political and economic insecurities incentivized communities to blame powerless yet undesirable scapegoats. By now, a theme has emerged: it is always ostracized out-groups who are targeted as Satan's bedfellows. Rather than being a historical anomaly, echoes of the witch hunts sadly persist to this day, as will be seen in Part Three's discussion of the Satanic Panic of the 1980s and beyond.

THE AGE OF ENLIGHTENMENT

Sociopolitical changes in the seventeenth and eighteenth centuries once again shifted the ways people thought about the Devil. A series of technological discoveries and the Scientific, Industrial, French, and American Revolutions all pulled violently at the threads of Europe's ancient hierarchies. Commercial elites gained power, and workers increasingly moved from Church-dominated rural areas to cosmopolitan cities.

While the majority of Europeans remained Christian, the idea of actual demons playing mischief with their lives grew farther from the collective mindset. And so began the age of reason, or the Enlightenment.

This secularization movement was supported by an emerging naturalistic view of the world, pioneered by Francis Bacon's scientific method and Isaac Newton's groundbreaking discoveries in physics and math. Scientists now postulated that the natural world could be understood through empirical examination and logical reasoning. Climate events, diseases, and other calamities of nature could now be explained through these objective techniques, rather than attributed to the supernatural.

Likewise, Enlightenment philosophers turned to skeptical and rational explanations for phenomena previously blamed on Satan. Thomas Hobbes wrote that demons were but phantasms of the brain. René Descartes held that the spiritual and material worlds were separate, and the Devil had no power to interfere in the latter. These philosophers criticized the Catholic Church's backwardness, corruption, and hypocrisy; Voltaire declared that Hell and Satan were among the many lies propagated by Catholics to keep humanity enslaved.

The Enlightenment period's novel attitudes toward Satan were accompanied by a rise of libertarian values, particularly rationalism and democratic freedoms (individualism, equality, and freedom of speech and religion). As a result of these ideas, the Devil gradually started to take on a new metaphorical association as a revolutionary hero fighting for egalitarianism and justice—a characterization that later became instrumental to contemporary religious Satanism.

FOLK SATANISTS AND THE AFFAIR OF THE POISONS

Despite widespread anti-Satanism and witch persecutions in Europe and America, there was no solid evidence of anyone engaging in actual Devil worship until the Enlightenment. During this era, a few instances of "proto-Satanism" cropped up in the forests of Sweden and scandalized the French court of Louis XIV.

According to court records from the late seventeenth and eighteenth centuries, some Swedish outlaws dabbled in a solitary and unsystematic folk-style Satanism. Since these highway robbers lived a life of crime, they thought it more fitting to pray to Satan for protection rather than to God. The bandits practiced simple folk rituals in the wilderness, such as asking the Devil to bless them with money and other material benefits.

Meanwhile in France, a group of soothsayers, diviners, and alchemists were thought to be dipping their toes in Satan veneration. In 1679, a fortune-teller known as La Bosse was jailed and executed for selling a deadly elixir to a client who wished to kill her husband. Soon after, those in her ragtag circle were arrested for providing women with poisons and abortions. All hell broke loose as others were accused of engaging in so-called Satanism, including members of the aristocracy. King Louis XIV brought back a special secular court called the Chambre Ardente (Burning Chamber) to judge those swept up in what was called the Affair of the Poisons. Before the tribunal was abolished in 1682, thirty-six people had been executed, and several others went into exile or took their own lives.

Much of the testimony laid against the women reads like a horror fantasy. Serving as a witness, an abbé insisted that an abortionist invoked the Devil by sacrificing a baby and pouring its blood in a chalice. The priest also described a recipe for killing the king that combined menstrual blood, an Englishman's semen, bat's blood, and flour. Others blew the lid off Satanic ritual sex acts, including perverted forms of the Catholic Mass that defiled the Eucharist, known as Black Masses. Even Louis XIV's mistress, Madame de Montespan, was accused of draping herself naked across an altar and drinking potions to make herself more attractive to the king.

While these testimonials were undoubtedly exaggerated, there was some evidence of lurid, unorthodox activities taking place at the fringes of society. Catherine Monvoisin, known as La Voisin, was a midwife who performed then-illegal abortions and kept a secret furnace in her home for burning the remains. Investigators discovered a chapel on her grounds, macabrely decorated with black drapes, candles made of human fat, and a mattress for allegedly conducting Black Masses over the naked bellies of prostrate women.

Although it is difficult to separate truth from invention, La Voisin's circle seemed to engage in some sex magic and necromancy rituals that veered on the side of diabolism. Their rites called upon Satan to help women who were abused by men or pregnant against their will, giving confidence to those who had little status or self-determination in French society. But authorities deemed the "weird women" immoral and persecuted them, as in the example of the diviner La Trianon, who lived with a female partner and had a human skeleton hanging from her ceiling. Today, some modern Satanists remember the Affair of the Poisons and its injustices by striving to defend reproductive rights and disempowered minorities.

HELLFIRE CLUBS

Later, in eighteenth-century London, the spirit of the Enlightenment roused some wealthy young men to rebel against moral conventions and adopt a libertine lifestyle. These "rake-hells" met regularly at salons to partake in drunken debauchery. The most notorious of these groups was the Hellfire Club, founded around 1718 by Philip, the first Duke of Wharton.

The Hellfire Club had forty or so members of both sexes, and they typically poked fun at Christian dogma in their Sunday gatherings. Members toasted the Devil and dressed up as saints or biblical characters: one woman reportedly stuffed a pillow under her shirt in a mockery of the pregnant Virgin Mary. These reprobates dined on blasphemously themed food such as "hellfire punch" and "Holy Ghost pie" made from an imitation Host (the sacred bread used in the Catholic Eucharist ritual). Once again, fact and embellishments intertwine, making it difficult to determine the veracity of accounts of these shenanigans.

In 1721, King George I issued an order that banned the Hellfire Club and similar societies, condemning them for stirring the flames of social immorality. Nonetheless, dissolute salons popped up in Ireland in the 1730s, along with rumors of blasphemies and orgies. Irish hellions were said to drink whiskey mixed with butter and sulfur, hold mock crucifixions, and conduct meetings chaired by a large black cat who was none other than the Devil himself.

In the late 1740s, Sir Francis Dashwood set up his own gentlemen's club at Medmenham Abbey in southeast

England, which he renovated in a decadent Gothic style. (Officially called the Order of the Friars of St. Francis of Wycombe, it was only later associated with the Hellfire Clubs and became known as their most infamous incarnation.) The "Franciscans" entered through a garden teeming with phallic and racy imagery, including a statue of Venus revealing her backside. Inside, they could ogle explicit pictures next to the Holy Trinity or browse pornographic and occult books in the library. The club motto, "Fais ce que tu voudras" (Do what thou wilt), came from François Rabelais's sixteenth-century novel about a hedonistic Abbey of Thélème. Members strove to enjoy life's pleasures and pursue personal happiness to the fullest, a notion echoed later by Aleister Crowley and Anton LaVey.

For about a decade, the monks of Medmenham—who included top politicians and poets—indulged in debaucheries that veered into the profane. Word spread that the "brothers" and "abbot" had orgies with "nuns" while dressed in religious costumes. Dashwood perhaps jokingly gave the Eucharist to a baboon, but it is highly unlikely that the men conducted Satanic Black Masses and baptisms, as some suggested. Despite the hellish associations, these Brits were not Devil worshippers, but rather aristocratic elites keen on showing contempt for established religion and morality.

"PARADISE LOST" LOST AND ROMANTIC SATANISM

During the early nineteenth century, John Milton's poem *Paradise Lost* (1667–74) received renewed interest, being widely read and praised and eventually awakening a literary movement known as Romantic Satanism. In Milton's epic, the still-beautiful Satan and his fellow fallen angels are banished to Hell but resolve to build it into a home and flourish together in their capital city of Pandemonium. In a significant departure from traditional literary portrayals of Satan, the author gave the antagonist a nuanced, humanized portrayal that reveals his inner struggles and defiant nature. The reader can't help but feel sympathy for the Devil when he avows it is "better to reign in Hell than to serve in Heaven."

For the Romantic writers of the nineteenth century, inspired by *Paradise Lost*, Satan became a metaphorical figure of identification. In their eyes, he represented scientific progress, rational critical thought, individualism, and emancipation—and therefore should be praised for rebelling against God's colorless autocracy. William Blake imagined Satan as a classical hero disconnected from a Christian context, describing Milton as a "true poet and of the Devil's party without knowing it." Percy Bysshe Shelley, Lord Byron, and Victor Hugo hailed Satan for embracing carnal desires without guilt, while Charles Baudelaire's 1857 poem *The Litanies of Satan* expressed adulation for "the most knowing and loveliest of Angels." These writers' works became known as Romantic Satanism, which, it should be noted, was a purely literary movement: none of the authors self-identified as religious Satanists or performed rites dedicated to the Devil.

Anatole France's later work *The Revolt of the Angels* (1914) further developed these themes and imagined that humanity's great accomplishments in art and science were achieved with the help of Hell's angels. One of these, Arcade, yearns to reassemble Satan's legion and overthrow the intolerant God who rules over Heaven as a martial dictator. However, Satan dissuades the rebels from attempting a violent takeover, as victory would simply put another tyrant in power. Instead, they are urged to break the bonds of religious authority by self-reflecting, pursuing knowledge, and living compassionately—ideas that many modern Satanists hold dear.

THE TAXIL HOAX

Two centuries after the Affair of the Poisons, another Satanic hysteria swept through France. In the 1890s, an anticlerical writer and publisher who called himself Léo Taxil decided to play a trick on the Catholic Church. For about a decade, he masterminded an elaborate hoax about an inner core of organized Satanists lurking within Freemasonry.

The stage was set by the 1891 novel *Là-bas*, which Joris-Karl Huysmans purportedly wrote after witnessing Satanic practices in the fin de siècle Parisian underworld. The book caused a stir due to its explicit description of a Black Mass, which had congregants coupling with altar boys and defiling the sacred Host in a writhing orgy. Quite a few readers were convinced that Paris was filled with clandestine Satan worship, despite there being little or no evidence of such activities.

Playing on these qualms, as well as on the Catholic Church's distrust of Freemasons, Taxil pseudonymously published a fictional tell-all about a theistic Satanic cult called Palladism. The "memoir" describes a covert Free-mason cabal that venerated Satan in shocking ways: Palladist nuns had sex with demons, and leaders plotted world domination through a demonic telephone system. Among Taxil's colorful cast of characters was a high priestess named Diana Vaughan, who later supposedly defected to the Catholics.

Like a contemporary catfisher, Taxil wrote books under different aliases that told the story of Palladism from dueling perspectives. He even published a photo of an unidentified woman, professing that she was the high priestess. One of his anti-Masonry works was adver-tised with posters bearing an image of Baphomet based on Éliphas Lévi's version, further connecting the Free-masons to Satanism.

Many Catholics lapped up Taxil's fantastical claims about Satanists and bought his books in droves. In 1897, he announced a press conference in which he would reveal the real Diana Vaughan. Instead, the author announced that the Palladist saga was a lie, and he was chased out of the theater by an angry crowd. However, the Taxil hoax was not a silly prank without consequences. His convincing tales laid the groundwork for later conspiracy theories about Satanic Freemason and Illuminati leaders controlling the workings of world politics. To this day, these lies continue to harm innocents that get caught in their web, as will be seen in Part Three's discussion of the Satanic Panic and the rise of QAnon.

FIN DE SIÈCLE OCCULTISTS AND EARLY SATANISTS

From the second half of the nineteenth century to the early twentieth century, France was the center of a flourishing occult subculture. Writers such as Éliphas Lévi (creator of the famous Baphomet drawing, who suggested that the inverted pentagram represented Satan) and Stanislas de Guaïta (illustrator of the goat head in an inverted pentagram) popularized symbols and ideas that influenced modern Satanism (see figure 2 on page 38 and figure 3 on page 39). This magical milieu gave rise in Europe and America to several groundbreaking spiritual groups that saw the Devil as a positive figure for the first time.

The Theosophical Society, founded in New York City by Helena Blavatsky and nineteen others in 1875, was a body of truth-seekers who investigated esoteric and Eastern spirituality. Theosophy's complex doctrine included the idea of Lucifer as a light bearer, a force bringing rationality and knowledge to humans. Fraternitas Saturni, a German magical order founded in 1926, similarly praised Lucifer and connected him to the planet Saturn. While these mystical groups were not yet examples of independent religious Satanism, they were among the first to admire Lucifer as an embodiment of enlightenment and reason.

Polish writer Stanisław Przybyszewski pushed the envelope further by publicly declaring himself a Satanist at the turn of the nineteenth century and surrounding himself with a circle of artists known as "Satan's children." While his Satanic ideas remained mostly literary, they formed a coherent system that put the Devil at its center. Combining an atheist philosophy with a social Darwinist theory of survival, Przybyszewski taught that "one must overcome Satan and become Satan oneself!"

A Danish man named Ben Kadosh published a pamphlet in 1906 that established a Luciferian cult and invited anyone interested in joining to meet at his home. That same year, in the Danish census, he answered "Luciferian" when asked his religion. Kadosh outlined a full Satanic doctrinal system complete with rituals for evoking Lucifer, but his "organization" appears to have been a one-person affair.

Then, in 1930s Paris, Russian aristocrat Maria de Naglowska founded an esoteric group known as the Temple de Satan. Satanism was only one component of her philosophy, which mixed Christianity, Occultism, and sex magic. Still, de Naglowska called herself a priestess of Satan, and bohemian disciples came to her for "Satanic initiations" into the teachings.

None of these precursors had a discernible influence on the modern religious Satanism that surfaced in the mid-twentieth century. Fraternitas Saturni has only a small number of followers today, while Theosophy has about twenty-five thousand members worldwide. Przybyszewski, Kadosh, and de Naglowska's organizations did not last long—but they are significant for marking the first instances of individuals calling themselves Satanists and holding Satanic religious values supported by some degree of organization.

ALEISTER CROWLEY

In the popular imagination, Britain's Aleister Crowley (1875–1947) tends to be the figure most closely associated with early Satanism. Although Crowley was accused of being a Satanist in his lifetime, he did not self-identify as one, let alone believe that the Devil existed. Nonetheless, his dark theatrical persona (he was called "the wickedest man in the world" and signed his letters "The Great Beast 666"), headline-grabbing profligate behavior, and vocally anti-Christian ideas had a resounding impact on later developments of religious Satanism.

Crowley's mother nicknamed him "The Beast" due to his misbehaving ways. As a young man, he squandered his inheritance on mountaineering and far-flung travels, and he experimented with occultism with several different societies. He visited Cairo with his wife in 1904, and she told him she dreamed of an artifact with a falcon-headed god. The next day, they went to the Egyptian Museum and found this very artifact, the Stele of Revealing—cataloged as exhibit 666!

The revelation led to a spiritual awakening: Crowley claimed a voice named Aiwass visited him and dictated

The Book of the Law, forming the basis of his religion of Thelema. The core idea—"Do what thou wilt shall be the whole of the Law"—is a variation on the adage used by Dashwood's Hellfire Club, which was in turn inspired by Rabelais's novel. The statement means that every individual has a life calling and should strive for knowledge and self-fulfillment while pursuing this vocation. Thelema includes a system of "magick" ("the Science and Art of causing Change to occur in conformity with Will") and a pantheon of gods, including Egypt's Horus.

Inspired by Rabelais's fictional Abbey of Thélème, Crowley leased a villa in Cefalù, Sicily, and established a commune called the Abbey of Thelema in 1920. The Thelemites scandalized locals with orgies and evocative rites such as the "Lesser Banishing Ritual of the Pentagram." Tabloids published exposés of Crowley's supposedly diabolical exploits alongside his sinister photo ops (a famous image shows him leering at the camera in a magician's hat, next to a black book marked with a pentagram). While most of his religious writing focused on other deities, Crowley did tip his cap to Satan in poems such as *Hymn to Lucifer,* calling him a noble and passionate spirit who "breathed life into the sterile universe." The occultist later spiraled into drug addiction and bankruptcy in the 1930s and succumbed to heart disease and bronchitis in 1947. Newspapers incorrectly described Crowley's funeral as a Black Mass because his friends read his *Hymn to Pan,* which hails the goatlike Greek god: "Io Pan!"

Crowley's eerie appearance and "magickal" ideas left their mark on the counterculture and religious Satanism of the 1960s. For example, the Church of Satan echoes Thelema's ideas about making the most of life's pleasures and using ceremonial magic to bend others to one's will. *The Satanic Bible* also reproduces the Enochian Keys, a series of nineteen incantations from Crowley's *The Equinox* periodical. Two decades after The Great Beast's death, it was Anton LaVey who would take up the black mantle of controversy that successfully drew in media coverage and put the Church of Satan on the map.

PART THREE

MODERN SATANISM—THE MID TO LATE TWENTIETH CENTURY

THE PROCESS CHURCH OF THE FINAL JUDGMENT

Modern Satanism emerged in the 1960s, a culturally tumultuous period in which many rejected the Establishment and "tuned in" to counterculture values. As ideas of free love and alternative spirituality gained currency, it's little surprise that the Age of Aquarius gave rise to the Age of Satan.

Most scholars consider the Church of Satan (established 1966) to be the first modern Satanic religion. However, it was the Process Church of the Final Judgment (established 1963) that initially broke key ground as a new religious movement that spoke of the union of opposites and the balance between Luciferian and Christian ideals.

Founders Robert de Grimston and Mary Ann MacLean met while volunteering as Scientology auditors in early 1960s England. The couple left L. Ron Hubbard's movement, were married, and founded their own human potential group. By the mid-1960s, it had transformed into the Process Church, which had a sophisticated Jungian theology incorporating therapeutic techniques and increasingly apocalyptic ideas.

Figure 7. The Process Church logo.

In its most developed form, the Process Church establishes four patterns of reality as represented by deities: "Jehovah is strength. Lucifer is light. Satan is separation. Christ is unification." Each is considered a fundamental force in human relationships and personalities. Processeans aim to find alignment in the universal truths expressed by these archetypes and reconcile the opposites in ways that transcend the component parts. Opposing the Process are the Grey Forces, representing conformity, hypocrisy, and mediocrity.

In 1966, about thirty members moved from swinging London to an abandoned salt factory in the Mexican village of Xtul (a Mayan word that means "the end"). However, a hurricane broke up the community, which then moved on to New Orleans, San Francisco, and other cities. Meanwhile, the Process Church presided over an all-night coffee shop called Satan's Cavern in London and produced a stylish magazine featuring celebrities such as Marianne Faithfull, all while proselytizing in the streets. Around 1974, de Grimston and MacLean divorced, and the church splintered, with MacLean's followers eventually founding the Best Friends Animal Sanctuary in Utah.

Processeans were frequently denigrated by the public as "evil Satanists," since members wore black robes with goat-head medallions while walking their large black Alsatian dogs. Some thought their logo, a cross made of four interlocking Ps, was evocative of a swastika. Due to rumors and misunderstandings about their secretive practices, the Process Church has been falsely implicated in everything from the Central Intelligence Agency's Project MKUltra to the "Son of Sam" and Manson Family murders. On the flip side, the church has had a lasting cultural impact (as seen, for example, in the album *The Process* by industrial band Skinny Puppy and the art and music of Genesis P-Orridge) and also influenced the vision of later Satanic organizations. While the Process Church was notable for its dark aesthetics and its Lucifer and Satan archetypes, it was another organization from the 1960s—the Church of Satan—that truly gave the Devil his due.

THE CHURCH OF SATAN

It is said that on April 30, 1966—Walpurgisnacht, the eve when witches are said to frolic with the Devil— Anton Szandor LaVey convened his Magic Circle of friends at his Black House in San Francisco. He ritualistically shaved his own head, put on a clerical collar, and proclaimed the founding of the Church of Satan (CoS). Thus began Year One of *Anno Satanas*, the Age of Satan. The first unabashedly Satanic religious group had arrived, setting into motion a philosophical tradition that endures to this day.

LaVey, who came to be known as the "Black Pope," loved to play up his origin story. Claiming a Transylvanian lineage, he was reportedly repelled by sunlight and garlic and had a tail-like appendage surgically removed in his teens. His self-professed youthful adventures ranged from taming circus lions to photographing murder scenes for the police and having an affair with Marilyn Monroe prior to her fame.

While his official biography paints a colorful tale, it is known that the "Exarch of Hell" was born as Howard Stanton Levey in Chicago, later restyling himself as Anton LaVey. He played the organ and calliope in nightclubs and carnivals, picking up the craft of carny showmanship that he later brought to the Church of Satan.

When he moved into a San Francisco Victorian home, LaVey painted it black and became known as a local eccentric with a charismatic Draculean demeanor. In the early 1960s, his Magic Circle of artists and counter-culture figures gathered at the Black House each Friday night for LaVey's entertaining lectures, discussing occult-related subjects such as H.P. Lovecraft's works, extrasensory perception, and cannibalism (rumor has it that a doctor brought a human leg for the group to taste). After the Church of Satan took off in 1966, many members of this Magic Circle participated in its govern-ing body.

In 1967, the CoS received a flurry of media attention for hosting a Satanic wedding and funeral. Newspapers covered the scandalous ceremonies, which involved such blasphemies as nude women sprawled on altars, inverted crosses, and backward recitations of the Lord's Prayer. LaVey also conducted the Satanic baptism of his three-year-old daughter, Zeena. Rather than burden her with guilt, the child was given sweets and attention to honor her natural instincts and lust for life.

LaVey published *The Satanic Bible* in 1969, and it became the central text of the Church of Satan. Over the years, he released several more books, three musical albums starting with *The Satanic Mass*, and a newsletter titled *The Cloven Hoof*. Dressed in a black cape and skullcap with horns, and toting a pet lion named Togare, the goateed LaVey was an enigmatic figure who thrived in the media circus, even claiming to have played the part of the Devil in the film *Rosemary's Baby*. He made celebrity friends, including singer Sammy Davis Jr. (who became an honorary member) and actress Jayne Mansfield (who posed for photos with him while holding a skull). When the blonde bombshell died in a 1967 car crash, LaVey suggested he had cursed her by accidentally tearing apart a photo that separated her head from her body.

In 1975, the Church of Satan underwent a schism: high-ranking member and US military officer Michael Aquino disagreed with the founder's direction and resigned to found the Temple of Set. He was joined by other dissatisfied members and LaVey's daughter Zeena, who later split from the Setians as well. (Incidentally, LaVey's eldest daughter, Karla, established her own First Satanic Church in 1999.)

LaVey became increasingly reclusive during the 1980s Satanic Panic that implicated his organization in evildoing. He kept to the Black House, watching movies and playing the organ for his new partner, Blanche Barton, and their son, Satan Xerxes. The "Father of Satanism" died of pulmonary edema in 1997, two days before Halloween. Today, the Church of Satan remains a prominent organization led by High Priest Peter H. Gilmore.

LaVeyan Satanism calls for the rejection of Judeo-Christian dogma, particularly the moral guilt it imposes. Members are atheists who regard the Devil as a symbol of individualism, pride, and liberty. They prioritize unlocking one's highest personal potential through ego gratification and the fullest affirmation of the self.

THE NINE SATANIC STATEMENTS

Originally published in *The Satanic Bible,* these nine statements convey the CoS's central convictions:

1. Satan represents indulgence instead of abstinence!

2. Satan represents vital existence instead of spiritual pipe dreams!

3. Satan represents undefiled wisdom instead of hypocritical self-deceit!

4. Satan represents kindness to those who deserve it instead of love wasted on ingrates!

5. Satan represents vengeance instead of turning the other cheek!

6. Satan represents responsibility to the responsible instead of concern for psychic vampires!

7. Satan represents man as just another animal, sometimes better, more often worse than those that walk on all fours, who, because of his "divine spiritual and intellectual development," has become the most vicious animal of all!

8. Satan represents all of the so-called sins, as they all lead to physical, mental, or emotional gratification!

9. Satan has been the best friend the Church has ever had, as He has kept it in business all these years!

LaVey admitted that *The Satanic Bible*'s eclectic mix of ideas borrowed from Ayn Rand's Objectivism (which values the pursuit of happiness and reason) and Friedrich Nietzsche's philosophies on self-realization. LaVey also drew heavily from *Might Is Right,* an 1896 social Darwinist treatise by the pseudonymous Ragnar Redbeard. *The Satanic Bible* speaks of *lex talionis*, or the principle of retribution: rather than turning the other cheek, "do unto others as they do unto you." The elitist ideology adds that Satanists are born rather than made: "blessed are the bold," for the humble "shall be trodden under cloven hoofs."

Some of these values can be seen as reactions to the mysticism and drug-taking of hippie culture, which LaVey detested. The Church of Satan does not condone illegal activities, and its Eleven Satanic Rules of the Earth (a list first circulated among members in 1967) include never harming children or sacrificing animals. The CoS has an open attitude to sexuality, yet dissuades making advances unless they are welcomed. Members take care to avoid the Nine Satanic Sins (a list published by LaVey in 1987), which include stupidity, pretentiousness, herd conformity, and lack of aesthetics.

The Satanic Bible describes our nature as that of a carnal beast, living in a universe indifferent to human existence. If morality is constructed, then why not "hail yourself" as the center of this subjective universe? Why not act in your self-interest and pursue pleasure as the Epicureans did, without falling into destructive compulsions? Bend the world around you to live your best life, rather than bending your knee to a nonexistent God.

LaVey's secularist worldview was based on reason but suggested that natural forces exist in the world that have yet to be discovered by scientists. In *The Satanic Bible*, he outlines Lesser Magic, or using wiles and tactics, such as seductive dressing and speech, to create change in accordance with one's will. By contrast, the rituals of Greater Magic create psychodrama to focus one's psyche, generate and channel emotional energy, and release untapped forces within.

The membership application process is detailed on the CoS website and currently costs US$225. The expressed purpose of such affiliation is to show support and philosophical agreement rather than to socialize, nor does the CoS engage in politics. Exceptional members may be granted titles in the CoS hierarchy, such as the Second

Degree of Witch or Warlock. The Church of Satan does not release its membership numbers, but there is no doubt that a great number of contemporary Satanists gravitate toward LaVey's doctrines and respect his legacy in blazing the path of modern Satanism.

SATAN IN 1960S AND 1970S POP CULTURE

While LaVey was forging his path of fierce individualism in the name of Satan, the Devil was leaving his hoof-prints all over the new media of the twentieth century. In particular, several blockbuster films and albums of the 1960s and 1970s had profound—and mostly nega-tive—influences on public perception of Satanists.

The oldest existing film about the Devil is *La Manoir du Diable* (1896), in which the archfiend is played by direc-tor George Méliès himself. Since that time, Satan has shown up regularly on movie screens—for example, frolicking with witches in Sweden's *Häxan* (1922) and ruling over Bald Mountain as Chernabog in Disney's *Fantasia* (1940).

The dawn of the "Age of Satan" coincided with the rise of diabolical novels and films. Ira Levin wrote his best-selling thriller *Rosemary's Baby* in 1967, which was followed by Roman Polanski's infamous movie adaptation. In the story, Rosemary (played by Mia Farrow) and her actor husband move into a New York apartment next to an eccentric older couple. One night, Rosemary is dimly aware of being sexually assaulted by a hairy beast with slit pupils. The plot turns to terror as she discovers that her husband is in league with the neighbors, who lead a Satanic coven and plan to claim her baby as their Antichrist. *Rosemary's Baby* introduced audiences to the plausibility of Devil worshippers living next door, shouting "Hail Satan!" while weaving nefarious plots to steal children.

Then came *The Exorcist*, a best-selling novel by William Peter Blatty that became one of the most profitable films of all time in 1973. Two priests arrive at a home to drive out Pazuzu, an ancient Assyrian demon, from twelve-year-old Regan. Viewers were shocked by the possessed girl's antics as she yelled blasphemies, spewed green vomit, and spun her head 360 degrees. Some moviegoers claimed to be so petrified that they fainted or suffered miscarriages. Worldwide, *The Exorcist* left a harrowing impression about the Devil's nefarious mission to harm the innocent.

In 1975, *The Omen* coincided with a growing societal paranoia about Satanism. The horror film focuses on Damien, an orphan who is in fact the Antichrist prophesied by the book of Revelation. He is adopted by a US ambassador and leaves behind a trail of mysterious violent deaths as he grows up. *The Omen* popularized the idea that the Antichrist could be walking among us and furtively manipulating politics—and created a devilish association with the name Damien.

As in the world of film, songs about Satan skyrocketed in the radical 1960s and '70s. But parents have long labeled their teenagers' music as "Satanic": jazz was known as "the Devil's own orchestra" in the Roaring Twenties. The following decade, legend has it that blues guitarist Robert Johnson met the Devil at the crossroads and sold his soul for virtuosity. (The alleged Faustian pact didn't end well for the musician. He sang of a "hellhound on his trail" and died at age twenty-seven of unclear causes.) Then in the 1950s, the hip-thrusting rock of Elvis Presley and Jerry Lee Lewis was derided as "Devil music."

In 1966, Mikhail Bulgakov's novel *The Master and Margarita* was published for the first time. It follows the Devil as he arrives in Moscow and, along with a naked witch and talking black cat, wreaks havoc on residents. Singer Marianne Faithfull gave the novel to her partner at the time, Mick Jagger, and it inspired the Rolling Stones' 1968 song "Sympathy for the Devil." In the song written from a first-person perspective, the singer is pleased to meet the listener, saying "just call me Lucifer."

In the 1970s, heavy metal took over the label of "Satanic music" with its thunderous percussion and aggressive and distorted sounds. Conservatives were shocked by Black Sabbath's discordant riffs and spooky aesthetics. Led Zeppelin was accused of Devil worship because guitarist Jimmy Page collected Aleister Crowley's books and bought The Great Beast's former home in Scotland. The *Led Zeppelin IV* album art also had occult-looking symbols for each member, which were mistaken for Satanic sigils.

Then, urban legends abounded about vinyl recordings with backmasking, or Satanic messages that were revealed when played backward. When Led Zeppelin's "Stairway to Heaven" (1971) was spun in reverse, those with overactive imaginations insisted they could hear: "Here's to my sweet Satan... He'll give you 666." Shock musicians such as KISS and Alice Cooper played up to the hype with nightmarish stage shows, and throwing the "sign of the horns" became widespread among rockers.

Ironically, most of the fearmongering public was oblivious to the works that were actually connected to Satanism. Anton LaVey released several albums, and the female-fronted band Coven pioneered occult rock with songs such as "Satanic Mass" and "Dignitaries of Hell." Avant-garde filmmaker Kenneth Anger, who did not identify as a Satanist but was close with the Church of Satan, created the erotic and demonically charged *Invocation of My Demon Brother* (1969), with LaVey as His Satanic Majesty, and *Lucifer Rising* (1972), with members of the Rolling Stones along with Marianne Faithfull as Lilith.

Hollywood and the media had succeeded in painting a shocking picture of Satanists that became deeply embedded in the popular imagination. Over the following decades, heavy metal and horror flicks would not only inspire and be inspired by the culture of organized

Satanism but also feed the anxieties that gave rise to the social chaos of the Satanic Panic.

ARE THERE SATANIC SERIAL KILLERS?

One of the biggest misconceptions about Satanism is that it is a favored doctrine of notorious serial killers. Starting in the 1960s, tabloids and TV shows fanned the flames by reporting on even the most tenuous connections as proof that murderers were diabolically motivated.

Charles Manson and his Family, for example, are associated with the Devil in the popular mindset, even though there is nothing in Manson's frenzied delusions of an imminent race war that could be interpreted as related to Satanism. Nevertheless, after his followers killed seven people in Los Angeles in 1969, the media grasped at anything that could be seen as Satanic:

- ✠ Murdered actress Sharon Tate was married to Roman Polanski, director of *Rosemary's Baby.*
- ✠ When killer Tex Watson entered Tate's house, he announced: "I am the Devil, and I'm here to do the Devil's business."

✡ The pregnant Tate was stabbed to death by Watson and Susan Atkins, who had been a stripper in LaVey's Topless Witches Revue before joining the Family.

✡ Another Manson killer, Bobby Beausoleil, played Lucifer in Kenneth Anger's *Invocation of My Demon Brother* and scored the soundtrack for *Lucifer Rising* from his jail cell.

Reporters fixated on these lurid links, describing the Manson Family as "Satan's hippies." Manson himself enjoyed adding fuel to the fire, even saying he and Robert de Grimston of the Process Church were "one and the same." (However, Manson also identified himself with Christ, or Man's Son.) Manson had once lived on the same street as the Process Church and was interviewed for the church's magazine, but all other connections to the group were products of pure mythmaking.

Similarly, shoddy reporting conflated the serial murders of David Berkowitz with Satanism. In a 1977 letter to the New York police, the "Son of Sam" wrote: "I am the monster Beelzebub, the chubby Behemouth [*sic*]." Ultimately, however, Berkowitz blamed his neighbor's dog for ordering him to kill. Journalist Maury Terry made farfetched speculations that Berkowitz was tied to a Satanic cult, once again scapegoating the Process Church without any legitimate evidence.

In some cases, Satanic iconography was adopted by psychopathic individuals:

✤ Between 1984 and 1985, Richard Ramirez committed a wave of brutal murders and rapes in California. Using lipstick, the "Night Stalker" drew pentagrams on walls and the leg of a victim. In court, Ramirez held up his hand to reveal a pentagram scrawled on his palm, and after pleading not guilty, he hollered, "Hail Satan."

✤ In 1984, Ricky Kasso ("The Acid King") screamed "Say you love Satan!" as he stabbed a teenager who stole some of his PCP. He and two fellow delinquents buried the body, leading to rumors that they had committed a sacrificial rite as members of a Satanic cult.

✤ From 1985 to 1986, Sean Sellers killed his mother, his stepfather, and a convenience store clerk in Oklahoma. Sellers later told talk show hosts such as Geraldo Rivera that these were human sacrifices to prove allegiance to Satan and gain personal power.

✡ Norwegian black metal, an extreme heavy metal genre characterized by rapid percussion and shrieking vocals, emerged in the early 1990s. Bands such as Mayhem raised hell with their corpse-like makeup, self-harm onstage, and hate-filled lyrics about the Devil. The Scandinavian movement was tied to church burnings, suicides, and two murders by stabbing.

Ramirez had supposedly met LaVey in passing, and Sellers and Kasso certainly had some familiarity with *The Satanic Bible.* Nevertheless, their ad hoc ideas about the Devil seem to have been based on pure provocation, rather than the affirmative values expressed by religious Satanists. None of these adjudged "Satanic killers" were working with a larger occult network as conspiracy theorists claimed. Rather, these killers had long histories of trauma and substance abuse, ultimately borrowing from Satanic ideas and iconography to evoke fear and provide a rationale for their crimes.

It is unfortunate that exceptional cases such as these tend to take the spotlight in conversations about Satanism. Far from being harmless, such delusions propagated the Satanic Panic, a misguided movement that ruined innocent lives through unfounded yet persuasive claims of Devil-worshipping criminals.

SATANIC PANIC AND RITUAL ABUSE

Much like the medieval witch hunts, the Satanic Panic sprouted from seeds planted in the public mindset by contemporary social anxieties. The 1960s and 1970s were a period of upheaval for gender roles: women's liberation movements and the Pill coincided with a rise in divorce and single motherhood. Some working mothers were made to feel guilty for relying on day care, and movies such as *Rosemary's Baby* and *The Exorcist* expressed a growing unease about the corruption of children.

By the late 1970s, Christian fundamentalists had become vocal about reasserting traditional family values. President Ronald Reagan spoke to their concerns in the early 1980s, and the antiabortion crusade ramped up, along with news coverage about missing children and urban legends about razor blades in Halloween candy. As the saying goes, "the road to Hell is paved with good intentions"—and many religious leaders, law enforcement officials, and mental health professionals genuinely wished to help those struggling with child-rearing. However, a flurry of misguided ideas and actions bred conspiracies about baby-sacrificing Satanic cults, resulting in a devastating moral panic that peaked in the 1980s and 1990s.

Michelle Remembers, a 1980 book coauthored by Dr. Lawrence Pazder of Victoria, Canada, and his patient Michelle Smith, lit the spark. Smith went to see the psychiatrist because she was depressed after suffering a miscarriage. According to Pazder, after months of sessions under hypnosis, she began to reveal repressed memories of a horrific childhood, during which she was abused by a murderous Satanic cult. Smith claimed to have been forced into sadistic orgies in a black room lit with candles, where Satanists made her defecate on a crucifix and the Bible. Her recollections culminated with the Feast of the Beast, in which each member threw a dead baby onto a pile and cut off the middle finger of their left hand. Then, the Devil himself appeared and preached to his acolytes.

Michelle Remembers became a best seller, and Smith's so-called recovered memories were taken by many as the truth. Smith and Pazder divorced their respective spouses and married each other, embarking on a successful lecture circuit. On daytime talk shows, Pazder described what he termed "ritualized abuse," or assault combined with ceremonies and symbols designed to invoke malevolent effects. The book's fantastical claims have now been debunked, but at the time, they popularized the idea that child abuse was a central objective of Satanists who had secretly infiltrated every aspect of society—including day care centers, where youngsters were easy prey.

A wave of false child abuse charges then surfaced in 1982 in Kern County, California. A woman diagnosed with acute paranoid schizophrenia accused four adults of molesting her two young step-granddaughters. Although no evidence was ever found, the four were imprisoned for more than a decade before their convictions were overturned. The hysteria spread further in Kern County, sparking additional cases concerning a "Satanic Church" running a child sex ring. Investigators asked dozens of children leading questions that encouraged them to spin fantastical tales about a network of Devil worshippers. At least thirty-six innocent people were convicted in this miscarriage of justice, and many spent years in jail before being proven innocent.

As Satanic hysteria grew, the McMartin Preschool became the focal point of what was to become the United States' longest and most expensive trial at the time. In 1983, a Manhattan Beach, California, mother (a diagnosed paranoid schizophrenic and chronic alcoholic) became convinced that her four-year-old son had been sodomized by his McMartin teacher. She soon accused other staff members of making her son insert his finger in a goat's anus and drink the blood of a freshly killed baby. Investigating police sent a form letter to about two hundred parents, suggesting that their children may have been sexually abused. The adults panicked, and local TV stations escalated the paranoia by reporting on the allegations as "news."

An unlicensed psychotherapist interrogated the students with leading questions and coercive techniques, including presenting them with "anatomically correct" dolls to indicate what had been done to them. Prompted by authority figures, the children told stories about being taken into underground tunnels by their teachers, where they witnessed infant sacrifices and ritualized Satanic sex acts. (The preschool did not even have a basement, let alone secret passages.) Pazder arrived as a consultant and legitimized these now-discredited interviewing methods. In his view, the children were always to be believed—and those who denied abuse were simply repressing their traumatic memories of the acts.

As difficult as it is to believe now, these ludicrous accusations led to the arrest of seven McMartin employees and associates. Seven years after the initial allegations, the costly prosecution ended with no convictions. Sadly, the damage had been done: one male teacher spent five years behind bars, while others had their lives turned into a living hell through home searches and media exposés, coupled with financial and reputational ruin.

The ritual sex abuse conspiracies of the 1980s were linked to concurrent rumors about Satanists, which were promoted by law-and-order conservatives and some Christian media outlets:

✠ Ozzy Osbourne and Judas Priest were sued for putting subliminal, demoniacal messages in their songs that allegedly caused several teenagers to commit suicide. Although the cases were thrown out, the idea of Satanic brainwashing through music stuck.

- Dead livestock were discovered with missing eyes, genitals, and blood—and some insisted that this was the gory work of Satanists. In fact, these "ritualistic cattle mutilations" were explained by natural decomposition and predatory or scavenging animals.
- Thousands of consumers boycotted Procter & Gamble for purportedly being in league with the Church of Satan. Their logo, a bearded man in a moon with thirteen stars, was thought to represent the Devil, complete with "horns" and a hidden 666 in his hair. It dated to the nineteenth century and had no such connection, but regardless, P&G caved to the pressure and changed the design.

The Satanic scare was further exacerbated and legitimized by the police and the Federal Bureau of Investigation (FBI). "Cult cops" held seminars to push the message that Devil worship had become endemic in small-town America. They passed out "educational" materials with tips on how to spot a budding Satanist: Beware if you discover a cassette by Slayer or Metallica!

Watch out if your preteen role-plays with Dungeons & Dragons or owns a Ouija board!

Some politicians and TV talk show hosts played up these baseless stories because the emotional reaction to the concept of Satanism brought in votes and money. The US news program *20/20* ran an influential segment, "The Devil Worshippers," in 1985. Three years later, nearly twenty million tuned in to Geraldo Rivera's special *Devil Worship: Exposing Satan's Underground.* The mustachioed host suggested there were one million "multigenerational" Satanists in America linked in a highly organized, shadowy network. Presented as factual reports, these programs glossed over the question of whether or not the Devil existed—instead hyping up the fearsome possibility that heavy metal–loving teens could be persuaded to do evil in his infernal name.

Phil Donahue, Oprah Winfrey, and Sally Jessy Raphael followed suit with "investigations" into what they called a growing Satanic menace. Talking heads such as Ted Gunderson, the former Los Angeles FBI chief turned conspiracy theorist, became regular commentators and were perceived as credible authorities. Housewives with permed hair also popped up on small screens, claiming to be "breeders" forced to give birth to babies who were then used in Satanic rites. When skeptics asked for proof, the women conveniently were unable to comply because those newborns had been chopped up and burned or tossed into the ocean.

In 1989, police raided a ranch used by drug smugglers in Matamoros, Mexico. They stumbled into a scene straight out of a slasher movie: fifteen mutilated corpses, body parts in kettles, and pieces of human brain in a cauldron. The criminals had been engaging in a warped version of an Afro-Cuban religion called Palo Mayombe. Nevertheless, daytime television shows described the Matamoros killings as cannibalistic murders by a Devil-worshipping drug cult. "Experts" warned that "Satanic killings" like these would soon appear in the United States, and many TV viewers took these so-called experts at their word.

Much as in the Salem witch trials, mounting anxieties led to the unjust prosecution of those on the fringes of mainstream society, such as in the case of the West Memphis Three. Three Arkansas teenagers who enjoyed heavy metal music were accused of murdering three boys as part of a Satanic ritual in 1993. Despite the dearth of physical evidence and what was later deemed juror misconduct and emotional bias, two of the teens received life imprisonment and one was sentenced to death. The West Memphis Three served eighteen years each before being released under plea bargains.

The Satanic Panic began to lose steam in the 1990s. The British government examined eighty-four cases of "ritual abuse" in 1993 and determined that organized Satanism was not to blame for any of them. Two years later, Rivera apologized on the air for his sloppy reporting about Satanists. ("I was terribly wrong," he admitted, "and many innocent people were convicted and went to prison as a result.")

However, the damage had been done: the Panic disseminated ideas about the "dangers" of Satanism that still survive today. In one particularly egregious example, an organization called the International Society for the Study of Trauma and Dissociation persists in promoting discredited psychiatric techniques, such as hypnotherapy, to recover traumatic memories of Satanic abuse. To fight back, The Satanic Temple launched Grey Faction, an initiative that exposes therapists who propagate these dangerous pseudoscientific theories.

Although the histrionics quieted down after the mid-1990s, the Satanic Panic did not end. Echoes of those conspiracy theories persist to this day, now further amplified by social media and the internet. The Pizzagate scandal of 2016 was a prime example. Internet trolls spread a rumor about leaked emails revealing that prominent Democrats—including Hillary Clinton—supposedly belonged to a Satanic global cabal of elites. She and other New World Order politicians purportedly met in the basement of Comet Ping Pong pizzeria in Washington, DC, where they engaged in ritual abuse and operated an international child-sex-trafficking ring. These delusional claims turned out to have dire consequences, with the staff receiving death threats and a gunman showing up and firing a shot inside the pizza restaurant.

In 2017, an anonymous 4chan user using the handle Q began to post "insider knowledge" about a vast child-molesting ring involving liberal politicians, celebrities, and world leaders who secretly worshipped the horned one. Before long, these QAnon "drops" included fake news such as the following items:

- Hollywood stars and Democrats were subjecting children to Satanic Ritual Abuse and harvesting the chemical compound adrenochrome from their blood, to use as a drug or elixir of youth.

- These Satanic pedophiles also trafficked and killed children in a shadowy worldwide network.

- In a subliminal hailing of Satan, the 2020 Democratic National Convention logo (a star in two colors) was designed to resemble the Sigil of Baphomet.

- The COVID-19 vaccine contained luciferase (enzymes that produce bioluminescence) along with 5G-tracking microchips.

Farfetched as they may seem, these hoaxes have taken hold of a significant number of people and continue to mar the public's perception of Satanism. On the other hand, some Satanists have begun countering this narrative by engaging in social action—most strikingly through the newsworthy campaigns of The Satanic Temple.

PART FOUR

SATANISM TODAY— THE TWENTY-FIRST CENTURY

THE SATANIC TEMPLE

Figure 8. The Satanic Temple's logo.

In 2013, a new group of Satanists arrived on the scene and turned public expectations on their head. The media began to report on a group who were shifting the paradigm through their "good works" in the world, such as adopting highways and cleaning beaches. These Satanists were lobbying for reproductive rights and lesbian, gay, bisexual, transgender, and queer/ questioning (LGBTQ) causes. Most notably, they were engaging in clever campaigns—such as trying to erect a goat-headed Baphomet statue next to a monument to the Ten Commandments—to challenge the predominance of Christianity in public spaces and establish equal representation for minority religions.

Enter The Satanic Temple (TST), a twenty-first century church that added an as-yet untapped element to Satanism: sociopolitical engagement. From its inception, TST has skillfully deployed both Satanic symbolism and grassroots activism to stand up for those marginalized by society. In less than a decade, members have created an energetic religious community and launched numerous campaigns that work to expose how laws are often arbitrarily applied to favor Christian interests in the United States (see figure 8 for the TST logo).

It all began in 2012, when Lucien Greaves (also known as Doug Mesner) and Malcolm Jarry met at a Harvard University faculty club function. They struck up a conversation about the potential effectiveness of a Satanic organization in advocating for religious freedom. If Christians could appeal to the religious protections of the First Amendment and Religious Freedom Restoration Act to further their moral values, then why couldn't Satanists do the same?

The following year, Greaves and Jarry had the opportunity to explore this idea in practice. Florida's Republican governor, Rick Scott, passed a bill to allow voluntary prayers at public school functions—so the pair traveled to Tallahassee to hold a mock rally in support of Scott, under the banner of what they dubbed The Satanic Temple. The satirical event featured a speech by a "high priest" wearing horns and a black cape, as well as a huge sign reading, "Hail Satan! Hail Rick Scott!" Supporters took to the microphone to express how grateful they were to the politician for passing the bill, as their children could now pray to Satan in school.

TST's cheeky rally garnered media attention and resonated with an unexpectedly large number of supporters weary of theocratic incursions into secular spaces. To most, it seemed that the Protestant governor had signed the "inspirational messages" bill so that Christians could deliver prayers in public schools. However, when Satanists claimed the same right to pray to the Devil, they were condemned by evangelicals. The rally showed how distinctions about religion can be hypocritical and politically motivated, and how many in power act as if the United States is a Christian nation when it is in fact a secular one.

Thanks to their headline-grabbing activism, some pundits have assumed that The Satanic Temple is primarily a political action group. On the contrary, TST was founded as a religion, and the organization was later legally recognized as a church by the IRS. Greaves has identified as a Satanist since his teens, having come of age during the Satanic Panic and having later studied neuroscience at Harvard, focusing on ritual abuse claims drawn out by psychiatrists using debunked techniques. Greaves reluctantly became TST's spokesperson and turned out to excel in the role as an articulate speaker, with his scarred right eye giving him a striking and slightly diabolical demeanor.

The encouraging reaction to the Scott rally assured Greaves and Jarry of the massive potential of The Satanic Temple. They immediately set about penning seven tenets to articulate TST's sincerely held beliefs and clarify its position as a nontheistic and nonviolent religion that rejects superstition.

THE SEVEN TENETS

The Satanic Temple has seven fundamental tenets that uphold compassion, the fight for justice, and the inviolability of the body:

I. One should strive to act with compassion and empathy toward all creatures in accordance with reason.

II. The struggle for justice is an ongoing and necessary pursuit that should prevail over laws and institutions.

III. One's body is inviolable, subject to one's own will alone.

IV. The freedoms of others should be respected, including the freedom to offend. To willfully and unjustly encroach upon the freedoms of another is to forgo one's own.

V. Beliefs should conform to one's best scientific understanding of the world. One should take care never to distort scientific facts to fit one's beliefs.

VI. People are fallible. If one makes a mistake, one should do one's best to rectify it and resolve any harm that might have been caused.

VII. Every tenet is a guiding principle designed to inspire nobility in action and thought. The spirit of compassion, wisdom, and justice should always prevail over the written or spoken word.

The Seven Tenets are based on Enlightenment values of liberty, equality, and science-based rationalism. Taking inspiration from the works of the Romantic writers and Anatole France's *The Revolt of the Angels*, members consider Satan a metaphor for rebelling against arbitrary authority and defending individual freedom. Anyone can join TST for free by signing up to be on the organization's mailing list (membership cards and certificates are available for purchase but are not required). As of this writing, more than six hundred thousand subscribe and are free to choose how they wish to engage; they do not have to participate in specific activities to be members.

Like the Church of Satan, The Satanic Temple champions personal autonomy and opposes decisions based on blind faith. However, TST disagrees with the more social Darwinist aspects of LaVey's doctrine, as well as the supernatural leanings of ceremonial magic and what TST considers organizational elitism. For TST, self-determination is meaningful when it goes hand in hand with real-world action to pursue justice and build community.

Unlike the present-day CoS, The Satanic Temple has active congregations and a physical headquarters in Salem, Massachusetts, and works on a variety of campaigns and lawsuits. In contrast, the Church of Satan takes the position that there is no place for Satanism in politics and that the CoS alone represents authentic Satanism. The two religions have been at odds ever since TST's founding, with tensions flaring whenever misinformed members of the general public confuse the two.

As TST's ideas spread rapidly through the internet and social media, dozens of congregations sprouted up in the United States, the United Kingdom, Canada, and Australia. Members now work together on a variety of projects, such as artistic performances and charity drives, in addition to the witty activism that has kept TST in the news. These Satanic antics are captured in *Hail Satan?*, a well-reviewed 2019 documentary that brought additional attention to the organization.

Some critics suggest that an atheist group could accomplish the same liberal political aims as TST without the "Satanic" label; however, for these self-identifying Satanists, the symbolism carries essential meaning. The

Devil represents an organizing set of principles and shared ethics, uniting members as they embrace their outsider status and champion science over superstition. By demanding equal access to public spaces as a Satanic religion, TST has raised important questions about whether the United States truly is a free and pluralistic society.

LGBTQ INITIATIVES

After the Scott rally, The Satanic Temple strengthened its profile with a "Pink Mass" in 2013. To demonstrate against the Westboro Baptist Church—which stages antigay protests, including picketing the funerals of LGBTQ military members—TST traveled to the Mississippi grave site of church founder Fred Phelps's mother. Same-sex couples kissed over her tombstone, which Greaves then tea-bagged in a tongue-in-cheek ritual to turn the deceased "gay in the afterlife." If Westboro followers could claim that their anti-LGBTQ beliefs were infallible, then why shouldn't TST have the same inviolable right to impose their views that Phelps's mother had become a posthumous lesbian?

In 2017, TST took action when a Christian baker in Colorado refused to make a wedding cake for a gay couple. Because sexual orientation was not an explicitly protected characteristic under the Civil Rights Act at the time, the baker claimed religious exemption and was legally allowed to discriminate. However, the law also stated that businesses could not deny service to customers on the basis of their religion. Thus, TST called for members to order cakes praising Satan from anti-LGBTQ bakeries, as the shops could not legally refuse to make them.

SATANIC REPRESENTATION AND SEPARATION OF CHURCH AND STATE CAMPAIGNS

Much of The Satanic Temple's work elucidates how dominant religions can receive preferential treatment in the public sphere, whereas the "Devil's advocates" are often barred from participation when they claim the same religious freedom protections. For instance, in 2014, TST planned a Black Mass at Harvard, describing it as an educational performance to symbolize liberation from superstition and clarifying that it was not meant as an assault on Christianity. Nevertheless, the event was picketed by about two thousand Catholics who framed the event as hate speech and made no attempt to engage with TST in discourse. Unable to secure a venue due to the protests, the Satanists made do with a scaled-down version of the Black Mass at a nearby restaurant.

As many US state capitols welcome holiday displays from all religious groups, TST congregations have requested permission to place Satanic messages next to nativity scenes in the interest of religious representation. Over the years, several such displays have been erected, including a sculpture of a baby Baphomet and a large red serpent entwined around a black Leviathan cross with the words, "The Greatest Gift is Knowledge." Although all religions are allowed free speech within such open forums, some church officials have denounced the presence of the Devil, and a TST diorama—depicting Lucifer plunging into the flames of Hell—was vandalized by a Florida woman in 2014.

Then, in 2016, TST launched its After School Satan Club as a counterpoint to the Christian Good News programs in public schools and published *The Satanic Children's Big Book of Activities*, filled with cartoon goats and pentagrams. The program's curriculum focuses on critical thinking and reasoning skills and does not teach Satanism. Much to the consternation of Fox News hosts such as Tucker Carlson, After School Satan provides a constitutionally protected alternative to evangelical clubs that proselytize to children. TST also runs a Protect Children Project that helps public school students exercise their Satanic religious right to be exempt from corporal punishment in schools. To get the word out, TST erected a black-and-red billboard in Texas with the organization's goat head in a pentagram logo and the statement, "Our religion doesn't believe in hitting children."

In 2016, TST Arizona asked to deliver a nontheistic invocation written by Greaves before a city council meeting in Scottsdale. It begins: "Let us stand now, unbowed and unfettered by arcane doctrines born of fearful minds in darkened times." By law, all faiths have the opportunity to give an invocation before US city council meetings, provided that no one is coerced into participating. Nonetheless, council members rejected the Satanists' request, and TST promptly sued on the grounds of unlawful discrimination. Although Scottsdale had never turned down any other group, the court of appeals ruled in the city's favor, raising questions about whether the law was fairly applied.

TST's best known campaign involves its magnificent eight-foot-tall sculpture of Baphomet. Crafted by Mark Porter and unveiled in 2015, the 3,000-pound bronze depicts the Satanic icon—a goat-headed being with wings, horns, and hooves—sitting beneath an inverted pentagram. Two children stand on either side of Baphomet, gazing up at its face in awe.

That year, TST offered to place Baphomet on Oklahoma State Capitol grounds next to a Ten Commandments sculpture, in an effort to test the government's neutrality regarding religious monuments in public spaces. The state supreme court subsequently ordered the removal of the Christian monument, and so TST withdrew its request. The Satanists then asked to place the winged goat statue beside a Ten Commandments monument at the Arkansas State Capitol, to ensure that minority religions had access to the same privileges as the Christian majority. TST's request was denied, and so the organization sued on the grounds that the government had violated the First Amendment by preferencing one religion over others. In 2018, TST held a rally for religious freedom in Little Rock, Arkansas, that displayed Baphomet and culminated with a speech by Greaves. Fundamentalist Christians showed up to protest the event, along with gun-toting neo-Nazis. As of 2022, the Baphomet lawsuit remains in court, and to paraphrase TST's second tenet, "the struggle for justice is ongoing...."

REPRODUCTIVE RIGHTS ACTIVISM

As theocratic politicians have increasingly enacted anti-abortion legislation, TST has stepped up its fight for reproductive rights. By invoking its special privileges as a religion, The Satanic Temple has filed multiple lawsuits to preserve its congregants' access to abortions. Beginning in 2015, TST sued Missouri twice over the undue burdens the state imposed on its members before they could terminate their pregnancies. The Satanists argued that TST members should be religiously exempt from these nonmedical measures, which included mandatory ultrasounds and waiting periods, as they ran contrary to members' sincerely held beliefs. Both cases were dismissed without the actual legal question ever being decided.

In 2021, TST sued the Southern District of Texas on behalf of a member who received an abortion. She asserted that the state-mandated interventions prevented her from performing TST's "Satanic abortion ritual," thereby inhibiting her religious practice and violating her deeply held ideology. As TST awaits the court's decision, it has launched other initiatives to protect reproductive freedoms, including offering religious counseling services and petitioning the US Food and Drug Administration for access to abortion-inducing medications.

TST HEADQUARTERS AND COMMUNITY

In 2016, The Satanic Temple opened its official headquarters and art gallery in Salem, Massachusetts, a city that is famous as the location of the witch craze attributed to the Devil's doings. Anyone can visit TST HQ—a former Victorian funeral home painted dark gray—to see rotating exhibitions by artists, attend events such as Devil's Dinners hosted by The Satanic Chef, or stay overnight in an ornate Gothic bedroom. The notorious Baphomet statue currently sits in a parlor, inviting visitors to sit on its lap and snap selfies. Another area displays the Belle Plaine Veterans' Memorial, a black cube with gold pentagrams on the sides (the Satanists commissioned the sculpture after the Minnesota city granted them a permit to display it in a public park next to a Christian cross—a permit it later revoked—prompting a lawsuit from TST). In the upstairs library, curious visitors can browse Greaves's extensive collection of Satanic literature, Process Church memorabilia, and materials on false memory syndrome.

While TST tends to make the news for its political action, it also runs a variety of community endeavors, including the following:

- Grey Faction, which works to protect mental health patients and their families from harmful psychiatric practices. Volunteers push back against licensed professionals who try to recover so-called repressed memories that further anti-Satanist conspiracy theories.

- Sober Faction, a peer support group that offers a Satanic approach to addiction recovery, without the dogma and pseudoscience that can linger in traditional twelve-step programs. In addition, Sober Faction provides a legal alternative for fulfilling court-mandated substance abuse meetings.

- The Satanic Ministry, an online program that allows eligible candidates to complete coursework and become a Minister of Satan. Ordained ministers can perform Satanic rituals, including weddings, funerals, and "unbaptisms."

✸ The Satanic Temple TV, a web television platform that airs live events, feature films, and a variety of original series that cover comedy, cooking, interviews, and more. Every week, a loyal following logs on to watch terrible movies and chat with Greaves during his TST3K Movie Night.

✸ The Satanic Estate, a virtual headquarters and online event space. The Estate hosts regular themed events such as Halloween revelries, an album release party for Greaves's band Satanic Planet, and weekly Temple Services led by a Minister of Satan. Guests can roam the digital rooms to experience lectures and entertainment and can interact by text and video chat.

✸ SatanCon, TST's annual convention, which first took place in Scottsdale, Arizona, in 2022. The event brought together hundreds of Satanists to enjoy speeches, vendors, and an Impurity Ball. Unsurprisingly, a group of Christians showed up to protest the event.

✸ Community "good works" led by local congregations. These have included park cleanups, warm-clothing drives, and "Menstruatin' with Satan" campaigns to make menstruation products available to those in need.

The political climate of the early twenty-first century undoubtedly played a role in the emergence and growth of The Satanic Temple. A growing unease about religious liberties in US public life, along with the continuing rise of globalization and social media, set the stage for a collectivist and politically active version of Satanism. In the spirit of Lucifer, whose name translates to "light bringer," TST remains hell-bent on shining a spotlight on social injustices and working within the legal system to challenge them. Much of the public still perceives the Devil as a malicious figure, but to these contemporary Satanists, he is a daring adversary who stands up for inclusiveness, benevolence, and empathy.

SATANIC RITUALS

In horror movies and TV shows, "Satanists" seem to devote much of their time to performing rituals for nefarious purposes, such as calling upon the Father of Lies to hex the innocent. Considering that most modern Satanists reject the supernatural, this type of demonic motivation makes little sense. Furthermore, many do not engage in ritualistic practices at all.

For those who do participate, Satanic rites usually function as acts of creative expression that help set intentions and affirm and liberate the self. Ceremonies may be privately held or open to the public and can be directed toward a broad range of goals, from celebrating a milestone to achieving emotional catharsis.

Consistent with the religion's emphasis on self-determination and antiauthoritarianism, Satanic rituals are never set in stone. Practitioners do not enact dogmatic ceremonies according to rote directives. Rather, the formula is flexible and constructed for a particular event or moment in time. Creative revision is welcome, and ritual structures are amenable to the personal preferences of those involved.

For decades, Satanic ceremonies have played an appreciable role in anchoring life events and commemorating occasions. In 1967, the Church of Satan received attention for holding a wedding, baptism, and funeral. In the funerary ceremony, LaVey read Satanic last rites in front of a goat-headed wreath and the coffin of the deceased, metaphorically committing his soul to the Devil while affirming his life. As for The Satanic Temple, since 2021, ordained ministers have conducted weddings at the Salem headquarters and other locations. Couples have said vows consistent with TST's Seven Tenets before the Baphomet statue, dressed in all-black Victorian garments.

The "Book of Belial" section of *The Satanic Bible* is dedicated to magic and three types of ritual that correspond to basic human emotions: lust, destruction, and compassion. LaVey suggests using devices such as dark imagery, chants, bells, scents, candles, and black robes to create an "intellectual decompression chamber" for focusing one's will and emotions. The "performance of Satanic magic" can thereby help practitioners manifest their life goals and desires and overcome enemies.

In *The Satanic Rituals* (1972), LaVey describes a series of group practices based on historical figures and diabolical events. One of these imagines a symbolic rebirth as it was supposedly staged by the Knights Templar, while another is an interpretation of the Black Mass enacted by La Voisin in the Affair of the Poisons. Participants in "Le Messe Noir" wear hooded black robes and symbolically invoke the Lord of Darkness by uttering phrases in Latin, French, and English. In one section, the celebrant picks up a wafer made from turnip or coarse black bread and touches it to a naked woman outstretched on the altar. Then, they dash the wafer to the ground and trample it while an officiant strikes a gong. For the Church of Satan, such rituals serve to elevate the self and generate emotional energy that can be directed toward a desired end, such as liberation from sexual repression.

In her 2020 book *The Devil's Tome: A Book of Modern Satanic Ritual*, Shiva Honey shares a number of mindful, symbolic activities that anyone can perform to attain a particular result without any supernatural context. These include individual and collective acts aimed at processing grief, improving anxiety, and enhancing interpersonal relationships. For example, Honey describes "Burn," a liberation ritual to be held outdoors during the waning moon with a fire and three lit sticks of incense. The participant can breathe deeply and reflect on negative emotions, writing them down on leaves using special ink. Then, the individual can throw the leaves into the fire one by one, stating "I liberate myself" while letting go of negativity.

Honey's book also describes several versions of the "unbaptism," an empowering ritual designed to purge the stifling psychological burdens that some Satanists carry from being baptized as children without their consent. At TST headquarters, she held an "unbaptism," in which participants hid their faces behind masks and had their wrists bound. Each walked up to the Baphomet statue to cast off the masks and ropes of bondage and to destroy an object that the person associated with religious trauma. "I abandon victimhood!" these Satanists declared. "Tonight, I destroy all gods placed above me!"

Some Satanists may put up an altar in their homes as a place for self-reflection and gathering resolve. The altar might include black candles, a Lucifer statue, a pentagram flag, or other items of personal meaning. No matter how rituals are expressed, Satanists who engage in them find benefits in the process and can use the results to effect meaningful changes.

SATANIC HOLIDAYS

Just as there is no requirement to engage in ritual, there are no mandatory observances of Satanic holidays. Nonetheless, many Satanists do engage in seasonal merrymaking, choosing to draw upon historical traditions and add their own devilish twist.

LaVey characterized Satanism as a self-centered religion, so he considered the highest holiday of the year to be one's own birthday. Celebrants are encouraged to thoroughly indulge themselves on their big day. Some Church of Satan members recognize the turning of the seasons marked by the solstices and equinoxes. Satanists tend to be fond of Halloween, which lets you express your inner self through costumes and also remember those who have passed. And of course, there's Walpurgisnacht (May 30)—the founding date of the CoS, as well as the evening when witches supposedly fly to the Brocken peak of Germany's Harz Mountains to revel with the Devil.

THE SATANIC TEMPLE'S HOLIDAYS

TST hosts online and in-person events for members who wish to celebrate their five annual holidays, which are these:

February 15, Lupercalia. Based on the ancient Roman festival, this is a day to "hail yourself" and revel in your bodily autonomy.

April 30, Hexennacht. Members solemnly honor those who were victimized by superstition, whether by witch hunt, Satanic Panic, or other injustices.

July 25, Unveiling Day. TST's Baphomet statue made its debut on this day in 2015. To mark the occasion, members affirm their commitment to religious plurality and justice.

October 31, Halloween. This is a time to embrace the dark side with costumes and candy.

December 25, Sol Invictus. Like the ancient Romans, celebrants mark the winter solstice with feasts and family gatherings. Some put a Satanic spin on Christmas traditions, such as by decorating a black tree with a pentagram on top or wearing playful holiday sweaters depicting Baphomet as a reindeer.

CONCLUSION

Your Own Personal Satan

Satanism is flourishing in the twenty-first century, and all signs suggest that the new religious movement's ideas will continue to catch fire worldwide. The associated motto of "no gods, no masters" conveys a focus on individualism, which means self-identified Satanists express their practice in diverse ways. Yet most are united in their regard for a symbolic Lucifer—the principled and spirited rebel angel—and find valuable personal meaning in their earnestly held spiritual values.

In Japan, for example, Satanists have a small but vibrant community that mirrors the country's distinct culture. Only around 1 percent of the population claims Christian affiliation, so most Japanese have little resonance with the traditions and symbols of Abrahamic faiths. As a result, residents generally perceive the imagery of the Devil as an "edgy" aesthetic choice rather than a blasphemous expression.

Despite this cultural difference, Japanese Satanists are as sincere as their Western counterparts in their nontheistic religious self-identification. Some resonate with the visuals and ideas of the Devil because they represent these Satanists' rejection of Japan's conformist social norms. IDEA, a Gothic and fetish bar in Kobe, displays "oni" masks (representing a horned and red-faced trickster from Japanese folklore) and holds Satanic rituals throughout the year. Similarly, other Satanists around the world might esteem devilish deities from outside the Judeo-Christian tradition that align with their own cultural experiences—including Santa Muerte, the Mexican lady of death; Yama, the Buddhist king of Hell; and Kali, the Indian goddess of destruction.

Much disinformation about Satanists has proliferated over the centuries, and such scaremongering tactics are still used today to vilify minority and outsider groups. (As Aleister Crowley put it, "The Devil is, historically, the God of any people that one personally dislikes.") It is my hope that this "little book" helps to shine an honest light on Satanism's long history and modern practices and to bring about a better understanding of the religion's core ideas.

Whether or not you identify with Satanism, there is wisdom to be found in its affirmative values that emphasize rationality, self-determination, and compassion. As the old saying goes, "the Devil is not so black as he is painted"—and Satanists have meaningful reasons to identify with the freedom fighter who courageously proclaimed "non serviam" (I will not serve). Perhaps Crowley summed it up best in his *Hymn to Lucifer*:

"With Love and Knowledge drove out innocence
The Key of Joy is disobedience."

And to that, I leave you with an exuberant "Hail Satan!"

SELECTED BIBLIOGRAPHY

Alighieri, Dante. *The Divine Comedy*. New York: Knopf, 1995.

Case, George. *Here's to My Sweet Satan: How the Occult Haunted Music, Movies and Pop Culture, 1966–1980*. Fresno, California: Quill Driver Books, 2016.

Demos, John Putnam. *The Enemy Within: A Short History of Witch-Hunting*. London: Penguin, 2010.

Faxneld, Per and Petersen, Jesper A. *The Devil's Party: Satanism in Modernity*. New York: Oxford University Press, 2013.

Faxneld, Per. *Satanic Feminism: Lucifer as the Liberator of Woman in Nineteenth-Century Culture*. New York: Oxford University Press, 2017.

France, Anatole. *The Revolt of the Angels*. New York: Heritage Press, 1966.

Introvigne, Massimo. *Satanism: A Social History*. Boston: Brill, 2016.

LaVey, Anton Szandor. *The Satanic Bible*. New York: Avon, 1969.

Laycock, Joseph. *Speak of the Devil: How The Satanic Temple Is Changing the Way We Talk about Religion*. New York: Oxford University Press, 2020.

"Lucien Greaves Is Creating Satanic Psalms," Lucien Greaves Patreon. https://patreon.com/LucienGreaves.

Mathews, Chris. *Modern Satanism: Anatomy of a Radical Subculture*. Westport, Connecticut: Praeger Publishers, 2009.

Milton, John. *Paradise Lost*. London: Samuel Simmons, 1667.

Nathan, Debbie and Snedeker, Michael. *Satan's Silence: Ritual Abuse and the Making of a Modern American Witch Hunt*. San Jose, California: Authors Choice Press, 2001.

"Official Church of Satan Website," The Church of Satan. https://churchofsatan.com.

Petersen, Jesper A. *Contemporary Religious Satanism: A Critical Anthology*. Farnham, UK: Ashgate, 2009.

"The Satanic Temple," The Satanic Temple. https://the satanictemple.com.

Stokes, Ryan E. *The Satan: How God's Executioner Became the Enemy*. Grand Rapids, Michigan: Eerdmans Publishing, 2019.

Van Luijk, Ruben. *Children of Lucifer: The Origins of Modern Religious Satanism*. New York: Oxford University Press, 2016.

TIMELINE OF SATANISM

Around 1200 to 165 BCE: "The satan" makes his debut in the Hebrew Bible or Tanakh.

Around 50 to 100 CE: Satan is given a more powerful role in the New Testament.

Around the first century: Lucifer starts to become known as Satan's primordial name.

520: The first known artistic depiction of Satan is a mosaic at Sant'Apollinare Nuovo in Ravenna, Italy.

1307: King Philip IV of France orders the arrest of the Knights Templar, who are accused of worshipping Baphomet.

1320: Dante Alighieri writes his epic poem, *The Divine Comedy.*

1486: Publication of the influential witch-hunting manual, *Malleus Maleficarum*.

1604: Christopher Marlowe's *Doctor Faustus* popularizes the idea of making a pact with the Devil.

1667–74: John Milton portrays Satan as a heroic character in *Paradise Lost*.

1692–93: Deadly witch trials take place in Salem, Massachusetts.

1679–82: The Affair of the Poisons rocks the court of Louis XIV.

1718: Around 1718, the Hellfire Club is founded by Philip of Wharton and is subsequently banned in 1721.

1740s: Sir Francis Dashwood establishes the controversial Order of St. Francis at Medmenham Abbey.

Mid-1800s: The literary movement of Romantic Satanism flourishes. Writers such as William Blake, Percy Bysshe Shelley, and Lord Byron reframe the Devil as a courageous rebel against tyranny.

1856: Éliphas Lévi publishes his famous drawing of the Sabbatic Goat, or Baphomet.

1890s: In Paris, fears arise over rumors of furtive Devil worship. Joris-Karl Huysmans's novel *Là-bas* suggests Black Masses are taking place in the city, while the Taxil hoax falsely links Satanism to Freemasonry.

1897: French occultist Stanislas de Guaïta draws a goat's head in an inverted pentagram.

1875–1947: Aleister Crowley, known as The Great Beast 666, raises hell.

1963: The Process Church of the Final Judgment is founded.

1966: Anton LaVey's The Church of Satan is born on Walpurgisnacht.

1969: LaVey publishes *The Satanic Bible.*

1967: The novel *Rosemary's Baby* makes a splash, followed by Roman Polanski's influential film adaptation a year later.

1969: Charles Manson and his murderous Family are dubbed "Satan's hippies."

1973: *The Exorcist* movie is released.

1980: The book *Michelle Remembers* popularizes the now-debunked idea of Satanic Ritual Abuse.

1980–90s: The height of the Satanic Panic.

2013: The Satanic Temple introduces a socially engaged Satanism.

ABOUT THE AUTHOR

La Carmina is an award-winning alternative culture journalist and TV host. Her blog LaCarmina.com/blog, about Goth travel, fashion, and Satanism, was featured in the *New York Times* and *Washington Post*. La Carmina is the author of four books, including *Crazy, Wacky Theme Restaurants: Tokyo*, and *Cute Yummy Time*, published by Penguin Random House. She received a journalism prize from the Society of American Travel Writers, and her writing has appeared in *Time* magazine, CNN, *Business Insider*, and *Architectural Digest*. As a TV personality, La Carmina has danced with William Shatner and Henry Winkler on NBC's *Better Late Than Never*, dined with Japanese monsters on Andrew Zimmern's *Bizarre Foods*, negotiated a $666 taxidermy head on Discovery Channel's *Oddities*, cooked cute food on *The Today Show*, and debated "bagelhead" body modifications on *The Doctors*.

She is a graduate of Columbia University and Yale Law School. Follow La Carmina's Gothic adventures in over seventy countries on LaCarmina.com and social media (@LaCarmina.